COFFEE IN THE CLOUDS

COFFEE IN THE CLOUDS

An encounter with the supernatural.

VITA MARIE KIPPING

Copyright © 2023 Vita Marie Kipping

All rights reserved.

No part of this book may be reproduced, or stored in a retrieval system, or transmitted in any form or by any means, electronic, mechanical, photocopying, recording, or otherwise, without express written permission of the publisher.

Publisher: Shine Communications, Saint John, NB Canada

ISBN: 978-1-7779362-5-9 (E-BOOK)
ISBN: 978-1-7779362-3-5 (PAPERBACK BOOK)
ISBN: 978-1-7779362-4-2 (HARDCOVER BOOK)

Cover design by: Vita Marie Kipping

Printed in Canada

www.CoffeeInTheClouds.ca

Contents

DEDICATION

EPIGRAPH

I
PREFACE

II
ACKNOWLEDGEMENTS

III
DISCLAIMER

IV
INTRODUCTION

1	In The Beginning	13
2	Man in White	21
3	Best Brunches	25
4	Daycare Dilemma	28
5	Chasing the Dream	33
6	Kitchen Praise	38
7	Wonder-full	42

8	Warning	44
9	Prophecy	48
10	Revelation	51
11	Shower of Love	53
12	Best-Laid Plans	55
13	Angel Care	58
14	Divine Decision	59
15	Sunbeams	61
16	Summer Fun	62
17	Creative Pursuits	64
18	Let The Children	66
19	Sidewalk Prophets	68
20	Beach Rocks	70
21	Summer Memory Books	72
22	Designer Treat Bags	74
23	Seeking the Sacred	75
24	Come Let Us Adore Him	76
25	Gifts of Friends	78
26	Goodbye to Summer	79
27	Friday Fun	80
28	Sunbeams Sequel	82
29	Holy Ground	83
30	Helping Hands	86
31	Rugged Cross	88

32	Sunbeams Service	90
33	Friday Finale	92
34	Dreams & Visions	93
35	Opening My Eyes	95
36	Summer Sunset	99
37	Work from Home	100
38	Foyer Fear	101
39	Little Flowers	104
40	Queen of Peace	107
41	Quick Switch	111
42	Voice of God	114
43	Pet Petition	117
44	Wednesday Wonders	122
45	Our Lady of Fatima	125
46	Guideposts	127
47	Visit Request	129
48	Saint Thérèse of Lisieux Novena	132
49	Morning Mass	137
50	Two Strangers	138
51	Show Hospitality	140
52	Fatherly	143
53	On The Right Track	145
54	Singing Over Me	146
55	Maintenance Check	148

56	Double Gift	149
57	True Presence	150
58	Higher Words	152
59	Coffee Invite	155
60	Skip in His Step	157
61	Stop to Smell the Roses	159
62	Litter Lesson	161
63	Hogweed	163
64	Like a Friend	166
65	Coffee Time	167
66	Back to Ontario	172
67	Desktop Image & Likeness	174
68	I've Got Land	175
69	Comical	177
70	Verification	179
71	Cleaning Companion	180
72	What's In a Name	182
73	Beauty So Ancient	184
74	Foot Taxi	187
75	Conference Buzz	190
76	Bible Drive	192
77	The Call	196
78	Conference Weekend	198
79	Spoken Over Me	201

80	AGM Invite	204
81	Retreating Once Again	206
82	A Meeting Like No Other	207
83	Divine Mercy	209
84	Quiet Time	211
85	May I Have a Word From You?	212
86	Do You Want to Know?	214
87	Floating on a Cloud	215
88	Keep Writing	216
89	Rabbit or Hare?	218
90	He Delights In Us	221
91	We Are Family	223
92	Holy Harmony	224
93	Love Can Heal	226
94	Do You Believe?	233
95	All Things New	238
96	Jesus Is	240
97	Confirmations	243
98	Important To Remember	244
99	An Invitation For You	246
100	Next Steps	247
101	Be Wise	249

ADDENDUM

A-1
DO NOT QUENCH THE SPIRIT

A-2
FINAL NOTE

A-3
AFTERWORD

A-4
SCRIPTURES ON HOSPITALITY

A-5
CONFIRMING ONE'S CALLING AND ELECTION

A-6
PSALM 45

A-7
I AM COMING SOON

Dedication

To the One my soul loves.

To my mother, Joan Beatrice Clark
(January 24, 1935 – January 16, 2023)

In honour of Saint Peter's Catholic Church, its parishioners and all who served or visited in its 133-year history, until August 2018, when its doors permanently closed. Although the church building was torn down in June 2022, a beautiful legacy of grace, love and memories will continue on in our hearts, minds, and souls.

And I tell you, you are Peter,
and on this rock I will build my church,
and the gates of Hades will not prevail against it.
(Matthew 16:18)

To all who have felt like strangers.
To all who have welcomed them.

In memory of dear Orbit, the happy, hoppy rabbit.

Epigraph

Do not neglect to show hospitality to strangers,
for by doing that some have entertained
angels without knowing it.

– Hebrews 13:2

I

Preface

This book came out of a true event that happened in my life on an ordinary summer day a few years ago—five to be exact. A simple *hello* led to an encounter that was both delightful and mysterious. There was something so special about that day that made a deep impression on me. I didn't want to forget it and so I made some notes to refer back to. Somehow I knew there was going to be more to discover about this experience. What was revealed to me is just too wonderful to keep to myself. This is a story of wisdom from strangers meant to be shared with others, including you, dear reader!

II

Acknowledgements

I thank God for my life, for all He has planned for me, for His care and protection, His sacrifice, and His eternal love.

I thank my family and friends for being a part of my journey. You have all helped me to grow in many ways.

I thank the strangers I have met along the way; each one a gift.

A special thank you to my first-born son. You opened a world of love and wonder to me and taught me many lessons along the way. May you find the Way, the Truth and the Life that leads back to your true Home!

Thank you to Christina Kipping, assistant editor.

III

Disclaimer

The descriptions of events, people and places in this story are real.

For privacy, names of people have been omitted.

There were witnesses and confirmations of the events I write about.

Please use your own discernment about what I share in this story.

Always seek what is best for you and your life.

IV

Introduction

For most of my life, I have been searching for something or someone. It has often felt just out of reach; a deep longing that will never be satisfied in my earthly existence. This is the human condition, expressed across millennia as each new generation grapples with the deeper meaning of life.

We are interconnected and yet often feel isolated and alone. We long to be known by others and to belong, whether it is with one other person, a small group or large social circle. We want to be understood, accepted, and loved. We desire to contribute, to share, and to belong. This longing begins in families and extends to include the neighbourhood, school, community activities, workplaces, service organizations, places of worship, and beyond.

Reaching out to others often starts with a simple *hello* and may continue with a conversation, and an invitation to share a drink, a meal, an activity, or event together. These moments create memories, which woven together create a beautiful tapestry of life. Sometimes these moments are fleeting but the memories linger with us long after. We tuck them into our hearts and minds as we continue our journey, sometimes recalling them fondly.

I am going to recount a story of a day filled with many special moments when I met two strangers. One *hello* and an invitation for coffee changed my day and my life forever. In the spirit of conversation over coffee, why don't you get yourself your favourite drink and settle into your favourite reading space? I will share with you what happened one summer day that will remain with me for the rest of my life.

I

In The Beginning

Like everyone else, I didn't ask to be here, but here I am mysteriously created and living on this giant planet earth, trying to figure it out as I go along. What do I know? I know that I am here to live out my life and to share my story—well, a part of it—in this book: the circumstances that led to an unexpected encounter with strangers. It seemed like an accidental meeting at first, as though I had simply stumbled upon these two people on this ordinary summer day. But I will get to that soon enough. To begin I want to give you a wee bit of background on me and the happenings leading up to that encounter.

I was raised in a traditional Catholic family of seven. My upbringing revolved around our family life, parish church, school, and community activities. I was involved with music, choir, theatre, art, school band, and piano lessons for many years. I loved drawing, sewing, music, and nature. At 18 I went to university in Halifax, Nova Scotia, the next province over, to begin an undergraduate program. I was originally interested in taking a creative, artistic program but well-meaning family encouraged me to do something practical and with the incentive of a sibling tuition discount, I soon found myself at the same university as my older sibling. I went with some hesitation but at the same time was looking forward to the new experience.

I really wasn't prepared for all that lay ahead. Slowly, the ways of the world were revealed to me and, being naive, bit by bit I was pulled in. It wasn't long before I stopped going to Mass on Sunday morning and turned my attention more to the secular world of university life.

After three years of taking courses, switching majors, and trying to find the right career path for me, I was feeling frustrated, aimless, lost, and trapped. My health wasn't good and I would get sick frequently due to several factors, including stress in many areas of my life. I felt like I didn't belong here but didn't know what to do about it. I didn't feel supported and didn't know who to reach out to for help. I don't even think I realized just how much I was struggling. I was trying my best to cope but on the inside I was feeling overwhelmed by everything.

This was a time long before there was strong awareness of the importance of understanding and having empathy toward others, especially if they were experiencing difficulties. It seemed like much of society operated on a superficial level without authentic care for one another. Growing up, attending school, and within society the message was one of self-reliance, competitiveness, achievement, and never showing vulnerability. Back then and for many years of my life, we were expected to figure it out on our own and it was a lot to figure out!

Asking for help seemed like a sign of weakness, but that is *not* true. Reaching out to others, including trusted family, friends, counsellors, and helpful organizations, when experiencing challenges in certain areas of one's life is what we should all be doing. It is an important way to love and care for oneself and contributes to our overall well-being. We can then overcome obstacles, set a new path, and begin to thrive.

I learned years later that we are not meant to do everything on our own, that it is OK to ask for help, that we are meant to rely on, love and support one another. This also applies when someone comes to us with their concerns. We must respond with love; offer our support as we are able or direct them to others who can.

Sometimes while feeling overwhelmed by stressful circumstances, I would withdraw into the church on campus and spend some time there. There was no one else in the sanctuary except me...and God. It was my quiet, peaceful shelter from my troubles, if only for a while. God was always there for me. He saw my struggles and He never left me. He quietly accompanied me and often carried me, though I did not realize it fully at the time.

> Do not be anxious about anything, but in every situation, by prayer and petition, with thanksgiving, present your requests to God. And the peace of God, which transcends all understanding, will guard your hearts and your minds in Christ Jesus. (Philippians 4:6-7)

> The Lord himself goes before you and will be with you; he will never leave you nor forsake you. Do not be afraid; do not be discouraged. (Deuteronomy 31:8)

A friend invited me to go to Toronto with her for the summer. She had another friend who had an extra room we could share in the house she rented with a few other people. This was the open door I was looking for, with at least a change for the summer. I quickly accepted and purchased a train ticket with my part-time job earnings. It was an exceedingly long train ride—almost 24 hours on a train seat that reclined a bit but not enough to have a comfortable sleep. But when you are young and looking for an adventure (and an escape), you can suffer through with hope for what awaits on the other side.

The big city was exciting to be in as a young adult. It was like exploring the world all within one city. Experiencing different cultures, new foods, music, art, local attractions, parks and trails, and even riding on the subway invigorated me. The vibrancy of this city made me feel truly alive and hopeful for the future.

Like all large cities, there was the darker side which unfortunately I continued to become more aware of. Crime, drugs, homelessness, alternative lifestyles, clubs and street corners where women were treated as objects, all slowly tarnished my view of this bright city. It is always so difficult to accept the way things are in this fallen world because we are all made for something more, much more. It was difficult to get settled and to find stable work in a huge, unfamiliar and expensive city that I didn't grow up in. I did a variety of different jobs including food service and waitressing, and then, over the next several years, customer service, office work, and sales support. My friend returned home at the end of the summer. I knew I was never going back to what I had left. I was determined to make a life in this vibrant city of opportunity and freedom and so I remained. I ended up living there for close to six years.

I finally found a great college program in the Applied Arts & Technology field and enjoyed the unique learning experience. It was creative, hands-on, and interactive, which suited my preferred learning style. I learned copywriting, graphic design, computer animation, photography, and other interesting skills. I loved this program so much and it was the perfect fit for me.

When you have the heart and mind of an artist, it can be difficult to try to fit in with typical careers. Our gifts are meant to lead us on a different path to bring something new and different into the world. It took me a long time of searching but I did find my path by following my deeper yearnings.

> Above all else, guard your heart, for everything you do flows from it. (Proverbs 4:23)

It was a time where I was still learning about human nature and the ways of the world. I was too trusting, and accepting, and tried to see the best in others. That sounds noble; however the reality is there are many people in this world who are not caring of others and are only looking out for themselves. It would be an exceedingly long time before I had better discernment about people and situations. Many difficult lessons were learned along the way.

> Do not be misled: "Bad company corrupts good character."
> (1 Corinthians 15:33)

After some difficulties with roommates, I resumed a relationship with my high school sweetheart who came to the big city to work and be with me, initially as friends. Partly out of necessity at the time, we moved in together, rekindled our relationship, and the following year had our son. Although I tried to make the relationship work and we were planning to marry in the near future, there were many problems and challenges, and much I had to learn the hard way. Sometimes no matter how much we want something, our life is meant to take a different direction. Soon, I was a single mother trying to make my way forward. It was difficult, but my son's sweet smiles and giggles opened up a beautiful world of motherly love that helped me to live with more purpose and direction.

After finishing my program and applying for many jobs in my new field I couldn't seem to get hired, let alone get an interview, despite my many follow-up calls. It was the recession of the early nineties and companies weren't hiring entry level staff. I had a stack of rejection letters that I held onto for a while thinking I might even keep them for my son once he was grown and looking for work. I would have the proof that it can take a long time to find a job. The stack could encourage him to keep searching and applying. I eventually tore them all up and threw them out thinking the constant reminder of unemployment was not a paper trophy I wanted to have displayed.

I decided to return to my hometown with the familiarity and support of family, friends, and surroundings. I took a couple of specialized programs: one on Entrepreneurship and the other on Document Design. I was soon hired as a Desktop Publisher at a company with a great salary and benefits and was able to use many of my creative skills.

After a few more unsuccessful relationships I thought I had found a kind, responsible and stable person. I had met him at a temporary job in IT before I got my permanent job. After dating for a couple of years, we eventually moved in together and a few years later had a son, who we both delighted in. A couple of years later, my partner had an opportunity for a promising career move in Toronto, which would mean me leaving my stable job to go with him. I had some hesitation and misgivings about going back to the big city but thought I would embrace the opportunity and see where it would lead. I was also curious about how the city had changed since the decade before. I also had a best friend from the first time I lived in Toronto that I had kept in touch with over the years. I was looking forward to seeing her again and spending time together in person instead of over the phone, through emails or letters.

The city was even bigger and busier than before and still had its exciting energy and vibrancy I remembered when I lived there before. I found a wonderful job as a Graphics Consultant and put all my energy into it. I also took a Web Design and Management course a couple of evenings each week which was interesting and exciting to learn. It was the cusp of the new communication technologies that would soon expand to much of our business and social interactions.

Although my partner had a great new job, soon there was talk of layoffs. It was a stressful time of waiting to find out if or when his job would be cut, and eventually it was. It was difficult to find a similar job with good pay but fortunately he was able to get his old job back in the city we moved from. I wasn't so lucky and had to quit my new job to move back but with no job to return to. My oldest son had to switch schools again and my youngest eventually to a new daycare. It was a challenging time and there were many stressors on us all. I almost regretted going to Toronto again but sometimes life takes these circuitous routes and we just have to journey along as our future unfolds.

We had discussed getting married, but it never happened for reasons that didn't make sense at the time but looking back were for the best. With a mix of regret and relief, the relationship eventually ended after nine years together.

Around this time I had begun work at a law firm and was getting drives from a co-worker. She was the only person in my life at that time that talked about Jesus. She was instrumental in me being drawn back to Jesus and to His church. I am forever grateful for all she did for me and for the Good News she shared! It was the hope I needed in the very difficult circumstances I was living through.

A while later, after returning to the church, I prayed a heartfelt prayer asking Jesus to help me and He did! A couple of months later, I met the love of my life in a miraculous way. We were gifted with a beautiful daughter and were married in our city's Cathedral. (I write about this in my first book: **To the Other Side of The World: In The Aftermath of 9-11**.)

We enjoyed a variety of pastimes together including movies, literature, music, art, and writing. We loved walks in nature, road trips, and our shared faith. We strove to build a life together and dedicated our time to our family, friends, and community.

We had been living in a large Victorian flat in the uptown area for a few years, when the elderly owner decided to sell the house due to health reasons. The new owner put the house up for sale again the following month, and then the third owner in as many months bought the house as an investment property. He announced to us that he was renovating the two flats and that we would have to move out for a few months while the work was being done. We were being given a renoviction with all that entailed. We realized we didn't want to go through the hassle and expense of moving out, only to then move back in a short time later. There was really no guarantee that he would allow us to move back in nor that the rent would still be affordable.

We began to look for another long-term place to live. It was around this time that the rents in our city started to increase and seemed to be above the value of what was being offered. Any that we found appealing were priced higher than our budget could afford. It might take some time to secure a nice place to live.

One day my husband came home to tell me that after attending Mass at the Cathedral, someone there informed him of an affordable housing program for families. It sounded like it could be an answer to our prayers of a new place to live. My husband got some additional information on it for us to consider. We would start with renting and then had the option to purchase. The townhomes were newly developed and although the area wasn't our first choice, we thought this was the best option for us at the time. We applied for the program, took a special course, and were accepted. After much searching, we finally had our new, affordable, and stable home.

The area where the townhomes were located was a bit rough; however we were happy to have the extra space in the new building and once we were inside we created a nest of peace and happiness. We were also close to a grocery store, shops, parks and playgrounds. We were within walking distance of a Catholic church. This church was connected to the school our daughter would eventually attend. It was a good start for our family and many great memories were made.

2

Man in White

My dreams never meant much to me. Sometimes they would reflect what I had experienced during the day, or something random, silly, or scary. I thought of them as night tracks; like entertainment or something for us to do while we slept. I had taken a psychology course and learned about the dream states, so knew some science behind them.

But then my dreams began to change to reveal what seemed like warnings, messages, and events to come. I began to record them as I thought they were not the usual dreams I had previously experienced but held deeper meanings.

Sometimes they expressed a desire for something in my life like the time I auditioned for a part in a play in real life and ended up having a dream about getting three parts in the play. I can still recall that in the dream I was driving in a white convertible with a boyfriend and telling him about getting the three parts in the play. I remember waking up after that dream and thinking it was unusual because a person only gets one part in a play, or so I thought.

The next week the director of the play approached me in the university hallway and asked me if I was still interested in being in the play, and I affirmed I was. He then told me that because of the way the play was written, I would have three parts: a young girl, a waitress and a saleswoman who would be on the stage at different times. That was the first time up to that point that a dream had come true in real life for me and it always stayed with me.

A couple of years later I had a disturbing dream regarding someone I knew. In the dream I was trying to run and hide from this person in a parking lot as they were chasing me and shooting at me. I was ducking behind a car, in fear for my life. I was looking down at the front of my body and seeing many bullet holes in me. I was bleeding profusely and was probably going to die! I was crying in my dream and woke up crying with real tears. I was deeply shaken by this nightmare for a long time afterwards. It was so real and vivid that I believe it was a warning. The years have confirmed this to a lesser extent; however I have always needed to be guarded around this person.

That was it for these very real dream "visions" until over a decade later, around the time my father died unexpectedly in the month of December. Within a couple of days of his death I remember having a very real dream of being drawn to look out a window. It was snowing in my dream and dark outside except for the streetlights. I saw a person walking along the sidewalk and he turned around to look at me and it was my dad. He gave me a big smile, waved at me, turned back around, and continued on his way. It was like a good-bye from my father, letting me know he loved me, and that he was heading somewhere (without me), but it was a place he was looking forward to going, and he was filled with joy about it. It was a reassuring dream and gave me a sense of peace and comfort.

Fast forward another eight years and I remember having a dream vision that was so vivid. In the dream I was being proposed to by my boyfriend who I had met in real life several months before. I remember clearly in the dream he got down on bended knee, opened the ring box, and extended it towards me. I recall this was in his living room and the lighting was dim. When I woke up from this dream, I was amazed by it, but I didn't tell my future husband about it at the time, thinking it might put undue pressure on him to fulfill the dream. The following year, he did propose to me...in his living room which was dimly lit. It all played out just like my dream. A few days later, I shared the dream with him. I knew God was leading me.

I only ever had a day vision once up to that point in my life. It was the day of our daughter's Baptism and I recall walking into my hallway and seeing a coloured stained-glass pattern just above the floor, far from any doors or windows. I knew it was related to the church where she would be Baptized later that day—the Cathedral with its magnificent stained-glass windows.

Many years later I had another day vision where I saw white rays coming out from a person's heart. They were similar to the Divine Mercy rays of Jesus, that are white on one side and red on the other, but this person had only the white rays, which represent the righteousness of a soul. This person was close to the Lord and this revelation allowed me a glimpse into his spiritual state.

A few years later and about a year after moving into our townhouse I had a dream about meeting Jesus on a beach. He was dressed in a white tunic with shoulder length brown hair. He was so peaceful to be with and attentive to me without saying one word. There were trees, bushes and flowers on the beach and everything was so beautiful. It was sunny and bright and the sky was clear blue. Jesus was quietly present to me and I didn't want to leave.

I don't know what woke me from that amazing dream but I think it was a sound in my home, or outside. When I woke up, got out of bed, and went to the kitchen for breakfast I felt like I was still on that beach. It felt so real and it took me a while to truly wake up from it and to come into the present reality. I recall mentioning it to my husband and he asked me some questions about the dream, including how I felt in the dream. How one experiences a dream or vision can often give insights as to whether it is of darkness or light. This was definitely one of light! It felt as though it truly happened and it remained with me from that day forward as something very special.

Around the same time, I had a dream of an older woman with some gray hair, about fifty years old, turning and looking straight at me and saying in a gentle voice, "You have been saved." The only person I thought this might be was Mary, Mother of Jesus. It was a short dream but again it seemed so real. It was reassuring to hear those words and it was an encouragement to do all I could to ensure I would truly find a place in the Kingdom of Heaven.

All of these dreams revealed important messages to me: something to happen in the future; a warning about someone in my life; reassurance after the death of a loved one; meeting Jesus and feeling His loving kindness and peace; being given a hopeful ending to strive for.

Some people discount their dreams but these dreams were so vivid to me—like supernatural visions. I always thought they were prophetic in some way, revealing deeper truths and meanings.

> In the last days, God says, I will pour out my Spirit on all people. Your sons and daughters will prophesy, your young men will see visions, your old men will dream dreams. Even on my servants, both men and women, I will pour out my Spirit in those days, and they will prophesy. (Acts 2:17-18)

3

Best Brunches

We began attending the church near our house, Saint Peter's Catholic Church, and enjoyed the welcoming community. The priest was a humble and caring reflection of Christ for us. The members of this parish were strong and loving and I could see that Jesus was powerfully present there.

They had lovely church brunches once a month and they were always a wonderful time of fellowship after attending Mass. In addition to the scrumptious food, there was sometimes a presentation or musical performance and always a draw or two, including a 50/50 draw.

It was at one of these brunches that I recall praying that we would win the 50/50 draw. We were struggling that month and really needed an extra boost. I really stepped out in faith and prayed fervently that we would win half of the amount raised by the brunch. The other half always went to church programs and necessities of our parish. After we enjoyed our delicious meal, the organizers began calling out the draw winners. They began with draws for other items that had been donated, then finished with the 50-50 draw. I heard the winning number called and looked down at my ticket. It was a perfect match! I waved my hand to let them know I was the winner and quickly went to the table to receive our much-needed gift.

It was given by my brothers and sisters in Christ who had all bought their tickets knowing the proceeds would benefit someone else even if they did not win. It was a much-needed financial blessing from God who I believe had answered my prayer. I was so grateful for that money and it really helped our family get through a difficult week. If God knows how many hairs are on our head, then He surely knows how much money we have or need. It was a boost to my Faith and to our financial situation.

> Are not two sparrows sold for a penny? Yet not one of them will fall to the ground apart from your Father. And even the hairs of your head are all counted. So do not be afraid; you are of more value than many sparrows. (Matthew 10:29-31)

During another Sunday brunch, I was going for a walk around the church hall with my daughter, who was about three years old at the time. After using the washroom, we were slowly walking back to our seats through the stream of people. In the hallway we past a delicate elderly lady sitting in a chair at the end of a long table. She looked directly at me and declared a simple phrase that struck me deep to my core. She said in a quiet, firm voice, "You know you can pray people into Heaven. I prayed my husband into Heaven." Not knowing quite what to say in response, I smiled and said something like, "Wow, that is amazing!" She then mentioned how she had received confirmation that her husband had indeed made it to Heaven. She seemed filled with much spiritual wisdom acquired through many years of living and praying. I believe this was a message that was meant especially for me this day. It was truly a gift of confidence and hope in the love and mercy of Jesus.

I had only had my reversion to the Faith a few years before. I was on spiritual *milk* and not the *meat*—more like spiritual *pablum*. Her wise words opened my spiritual eyes to God's amazing love that includes us in the redemption of His other children. It was a small yet powerful seed that she planted in my soul that day and it grew every week as I learned more about the power of prayer—for ourselves and others.

4

Daycare Dilemma

At the time, I was working at a museum in community relations and my husband was teaching drumming lessons and was also involved in local musical performances and projects. Our daughter was going to daycare Monday through Friday. I was working four days a week but we would put her in daycare Friday too since we had to pay for the full week. I would use that day for grocery shopping, errands, and homecare.

It was heartbreaking to hear my little one say with a sigh on a Friday morning, "Another long day at daycare." I would try to finish my chores and errands as soon as possible to pick her up early, but eventually I just couldn't drop her off on Fridays knowing she was just filling in the hours and not really enjoying it that much.

I also noted she wasn't learning much as the daycares had all become play based. I never saw a letter or a number sheet or anything else related to building a foundation for elementary school learning. Our young children's learning potential is being reduced by only focusing on play. Yes, they learn a lot through play but they also can enjoy and thrive through fun, educational programs. I knew she had so much more potential that was underdeveloped at this time.

I decided to keep her with me on Fridays. I would take her with me to get groceries and do errands and we would make it an adventure. I would often include a trip to a playground or park, a learning activity, fun and educational workbooks with lots of stickers, snuggling up to read together, and a small treat or surprise.

One of the local thrift stores had small bags of children's trinkets for a dollar or two. They were a mix of different toys, figures, craft items and other little treasures. They were easy on my budget but their value to my daughter was priceless as she got so much enjoyment from exploring them and playing with them in creative and imaginative ways. They were an end of the week surprise for her to look forward to.

These were special times spent together and I will always look back fondly on them. Not all the housework got done but much learning, exploring, growth, giggles, and precious memories were made—woven together with love between a mother and her child.

After more months of our daughter attending daycare Monday through Thursday and not really thriving, my husband proposed staying home with her for a year to provide "Daddy Daycare." He wanted to teach her more and have her experience a day filled with unique excursions, lots of physical fitness outside, and more connection with nature.

I was so grateful for my husband's generous offer to do this. I knew it would take some pressure off our mornings and we wouldn't have that huge daycare bill every week. We were willing to forgo some extras knowing our daughter would be more content at home with special time learning, and outings with her dad. I would continue our special Mom and Daughter days on Fridays.

We quickly knew this had been the right decision. Our daughter was immediately happier at home throughout the week and she enjoyed her special learning time and daily outings with her dad.

A few months later, we decided to enrol our daughter part-time at a nearby preschool. It was part of the school community that she would eventually attend. It was for a couple of mornings each week and had a small group size. The teacher was focused on helping the children to develop in all areas in preparation for kindergarten.

It gave our daughter an opportunity to spend time with friends her age, to learn more about a structured routine, and to develop new skills and some independence. It gave my husband a bit of a break during the week so he could have much-needed time for himself, for his work and his projects. All parents need this gift of quiet, time and space. It helps them to be better parents, partners, and people.

My husband continued his Daddy Daycare on the alternate days with more emphasis on learning. He made it a unique and fun educational experience for her and he began to focus on phonics with the goal of our daughter learning to read early. He found a couple of free quality phonics and learning based websites and he bought several preschool workbooks. Each morning they would focus on learning, and in the afternoon would go out for adventures.

The summer came and my husband continued to provide a fun-filled and educational program for our daughter and she thrived. They would often pick me up at the end of my workday which I much preferred to waiting for a bus. She would sometimes be eating a child-sized ice cream cone after coming from a swim at one of the area beaches. She would have messy hair and her face would be shiny with sunblock. She had a big smile on her face and a deep joy from being well cared for and experiencing a day filled with learning, little adventures, variety, and love from her dedicated dad.

In the fall, we moved her up to the four mornings per week preschool program in anticipation of her attending kindergarten at the adjoining school the following year. We wanted her to get familiar with the daily routine. It also gave my husband some more time for his work and music projects.

Our home was always filled with music, reading, interesting conversations, and learning new things. I always loved snuggling with our daughter and reading her a variety of books over the years, and this continued especially on our Fridays together. On one of these Fridays, I chose a simple, lighthearted book about a clown and invited my daughter to try reading it. I put my finger under each word and she began to sound them out. She spontaneously began to read this simple book aloud by herself. I knew my husband had spent many months patiently working on phonics with her and so the foundation for reading was there but it was still surprising to hear my little girl reading word after word, page after page to the end of the book. She was a little surprised too at what she accomplished that day. She was beaming with satisfaction at her accomplishment and it spurred her on to want to read more books on her own.

She learned how to read at the young age of four and it was a beautiful gift she received! She quickly began to read many books we had in the house or borrowed from the library. I would still spend time reading books to her or listening to her read on her own, but she now had the added advantage of picking up a book during the day and reading it on her own. She would enter into the world of the book she was reading with her imagination and was content to explore on her own. She was soon able to read short chapter books and learned at a quick pace.

My only concern was balancing her ability as an advanced reader with appropriate content for her age. I decided to research and compile lists of books for her and then borrow them from the library. Often she would read a book a couple of years ahead of her age but the content was still suitable. We truly underestimate what young children are capable of learning and I encourage all parents, caregivers, daycares, and preschools to consider teaching children to read early.

5

Chasing the Dream

I was starting to feel a bit disillusioned with my job. There were several factors contributing to this including a heavy workload and often last-minute assignments to squeeze into an already full schedule. I felt like I was still working a five-day work week even though I was being paid for four days as I often worked past my shift end time and sometimes came in to work on Fridays to finish urgent work. Every morning I hit the ground running and often felt a heightened sense of distress throughout my day. I could see it in many of my co-workers too and I began to wonder how much longer I could sustain this unrelenting pace.

I also had a manager who was sick and had been in and out of the office over the course of many months. There were days she came in to work when she would have been better off resting at home. I covered some of her work duties when she was too sick to come in which added another level of responsibility to my already heavy workload. We really needed an extra person to help with all the work, but that person would not arrive for a very long time.

I remember waking up one morning in early 2010 and feeling this sudden pressure in the middle of my body in a vein or an artery—in the area of my heart. I also had a queasy feeling in my stomach. It was as though my body was reacting to all of the long-term stress and was giving me a warning. I did call in sick that day and took a much-needed day of rest, both physical and mental.

I returned to work the following day, a bit reluctantly. I continued doing my job to the best of my ability but it was taking its toll on me. I could see my manager's health was continuing to deteriorate and although I tried to stay hopeful, deep down I could see that she was not going to recover. I don't know if she considered herself a Christian but I prayed for her many times throughout her illness. Harkening back to that elderly woman at my church and her wise counsel of praying people into Heaven, I kept praying with strong faith.

My manager passed away that summer after her long and difficult battle. I felt a mix of relief, sorrow, and concern for her soul. I can only hope that God answered my prayers (and those of others and perhaps hers) and that she is now in His peaceful, loving presence.

In addition to trying to move forward after the prolonged illness and death of my colleague, I was now doing the work of two people and it was just too much. My body was trying to get my attention and I continued to have strange symptoms of unwellness. I went to the doctor and was immediately diagnosed with high blood pressure. I knew it wasn't a good diagnosis and knowing there was heart disease in my family didn't help.

The doctor wrote me a prescription for medication, as well as a doctor's note for immediate medical leave. This was the wakeup call to me that I had to take better care of myself, which might include another line of work or at least a different pace of work. After a few days of rest away from the workplace and taking my medication, I started to feel a bit better.

After being home for about two weeks on medical leave, I returned to work. I was going to try to do my best and continue on with the job. But so much had changed in a short amount of time, including me. I began to attend noon Mass at the Cathedral during some of my lunch breaks. I would quickly walk there and back and eat my lunch at my desk while I resumed my work. The exercise, sunshine and fresh air was good for me too and receiving the Bread of Life sustained me through the weekdays.

Often I would walk home after work—a 45-minute walk—to get more exercise and to decompress after the busy workday. It was during these walks that I was inspired to design simple prayer cards and leave them in public spaces like buses, park benches, and store shelves for someone to find. I didn't realize it then but I was being drawn closer to God and the beginning of a special mission was being ignited in me.

I was also coming to terms with never having a permanent job at the museum as I was not bilingual, and that was a requirement. The schools I attended growing up did not offer French Immersion. I was always at a disadvantage for any jobs requiring both languages, which continued to increase each year.

My job was a contract only and it was very insecure. There was never any talk of anything long-term, and then the contracts became shorter, and I was often left wondering if it would be renewed for another term.

Sometimes I felt taken for granted and not truly valued—certainly not as much as the paintings or exhibits that were displayed as treasures. It seemed as though everything in this world was lacking a true commitment, whether relationships, marriages, friendships, or work—so much seemed to be transient.

Loyalty goes both ways between an employer and an employee—or it used to be this way—and it is difficult and unfair when it often feels one-sided. People get up everyday to go to a job and most try to do their best. Most employees are looking for a place to contribute their time and talent and to feel like they belong and are appreciated. With the faster paced technological world we are now living in, much has become impersonal. The world of work has been rapidly changing over the past few decades and not always for the benefit of everyone.

Although many of the stories of history and the associated artifacts, exhibits, and presentations were educational and interesting, I realized I was longing for something more. I was coming to the realization that instead of being interested in the preservation of the past, I was really looking forward to the future, not just on this earth, but what was beyond this realm of existence. I was longing to know more about the One Eternal God.

It wasn't long before the symptoms flared up again, and I took a second medical leave. I researched some of the causes and side effects of high blood pressure and what I read concerned me. It was also known as the *silent killer*. I didn't want my life to be *silenced* unexpectedly and too early. My father had died of a heart attack at his retirement many years before. My grandmother had died of a heart attack too though well into her eighties. I knew high blood pressure could be a cause. I began to think that I was going to be one of those people who is on high blood pressure medication for the rest of their life. I felt so much older than my forty-five years. I was having a bit of a mid-life health crisis, feeling like this was the beginning of the downward spiral of my health and that it might not ever improve.

I did quite a bit of research and uncovered a lot of medical information on the negative effect stress, including job stress, has on a person's health. I began to realize a return to that job was not going to happen. The 'universe' (but really it is God!) has a way of getting our attention and redirecting us onto a different path. The next meeting I had at the workplace concerned budget cuts and reduced hours and soon I was set free to pursue a dream that had been germinating in my mind over the past year—one of starting a home-based business.

I did a few short contract jobs to help with the bills but my health still wasn't good. All that had transpired in recent years had negatively impacted my health long-term and it would take a while to feel close to normal again. I did what was necessary for my health and each week I continued to feel better, until my blood pressure returned to normal and I came off the medication. Months later my blood pressure remained in the healthy range. My health issues were caused by job-related stress and being away from it, my mind and body were healing.

We sometimes forget that we are human and that we have our limitations. Even a computer may stop working properly and may require replacement parts or to be replaced completely. We as human resources must listen to ourselves and to each other to do what is necessary to encourage, support, and maintain a balance of wellness in our lives and workplaces. In our fast-paced world it is often overlooked to the detriment of employees, organizations, families, and communities.

6

Kitchen Praise

I began to research my business idea and would work on it in the mornings and evenings. The research and other business plan work was building momentum to continue to focus on the goal of starting this business. I felt renewed hope about my future, like I had been given another chance at my dreams.

My daughter was now attending kindergarten at the local private Catholic school, Divine Mercy Catholic School (DMCS)—the little school with the big heart—which was located on the same property as our church (St. Peter's Catholic Church) and up a set of stairs from the preschool she had previously attended.

She had an amazing teacher who really brought out the best in each child. It was a stimulating environment for my daughter and she loved it. The school itself was one that was filled with love and acceptance of every child. It focused on educating the whole child, including the spiritual, which is often overlooked but important for a child's growth and well-being.

The school had a mandatory policy whereby the students were required to wear uniforms. Previously when I would see students in uniforms in other cities I lived in or visited, I was a bit ambivalent about them. But with the introduction of uniforms into our daughter's life, I quickly learned their value and how easy they made our mornings. Monday through Thursday, she had a choice of a navy-blue skirt, skort or pants with a red, blue, or white polo with the school's insignia. On Fridays it was dressier, with an added blue vest, white blouse, and blue and red pin-striped tie.

The wearing of uniforms took the focus off of the students' outfits and instead put the focus on the character and value of the person and being a part of a learning and faith community. The students seemed to accept wearing the uniforms but would express their uniqueness in small ways, like how they did their hair, the colour of their socks or an added accessory. They could also choose their own coats, shoes, backpacks, and lunch bags. I thought the students looked sharp and smart in their uniforms and could easily express their individual personalities beyond what they were wearing. It definitely simplified mornings and made it easy for the children to choose an outfit that always looked well put together.

DMCS was a non-profit tuition-based school and they tried to keep the costs as low as possible. We knew it would still be a financial sacrifice for our daughter to attend but we knew it was a worthy one. We were so grateful for the fund we applied to for some assistance with the costs. Also, her grandfather helped with her tuition for many of the years she attended. This was a significant help to our family and we are forever grateful for his generosity. After he died, we continued to make sacrifices so our daughter could continue to attend the school that she loved so much and where she truly belonged. There were a couple of years where we would clean the school in the evenings in exchange for her tuition and one year I worked part-time in the office for a tuition discount. It wasn't easy but it was worth our daughter continuing to learn in this special environment of love, support, enrichment—and most importantly the beautiful faith.

The music program at the school was exceptional. The students began their day with chapel time which included praise and worship with songs, prayers, and faith teachings. At least twice per week there was Mass offered by a local priest and on special occasions the bishop. The children were infused with beautiful hymns, Bible readings, homilies, and the Eucharist that lifted their souls to the One who loves them.

My daughter would come home singing parts of these special songs. A line or two would be enough to make me stop what I was doing and listen intently to the tune and the lyrics. I recall going to the computer in the corner of the kitchen and typing a few of the lyrics to find the song online. I would then play the song and was often deeply moved by the meaning behind it and often an inspiring video to accompany it. I quickly discovered playlists and began to play them occasionally while making a meal. I would sometimes have it playing while I cleaned up the kitchen and sometimes afterwards for a while. The music stirred my soul and I loved to hear all the new and refreshing songs that Christian artists were releasing.

I recall one Friday evening playing one of these playlists and doing my best to sing along with my daughter. It wasn't long after that I felt such immense joy, almost a giddiness during this time. I realized much later that because my daughter and I were *gathered in Jesus' name*, He was there in our midst. God was in my kitchen! Also, *God inhabits our praises*, so while we were praising God through playing and singing the praise and worship music, we had invited God to be with us. It was such a joyful time and we would do it many more times.

> "For where two or three gather in my name, there am I with them." (Matthew 18:20)

There was a song on one of my husband's CDs about *putting on a garment of praise for a heavy heart* and I had previously wondered what it meant. I recall finding the related scripture somewhere in the Bible years later. Whenever I felt a bit down, I would put praise and worship music on and sing along, praising the Lord, and soon after the atmosphere in the room would change and I would change from having a heavy heart to having one of joy. To this day I still play this music in my home, praising God for who He is and what He has done for me and others, and it continues to transform the atmosphere in the room! It is another way that our home can be a *Domestic Church*. You don't have to limit yourself to your home. I've invited God into my car through prayer and praise. Take a road trip and invite God along!

7

Wonder-full

The time that I was working on my business plan allowed me to have some flexibility. I would volunteer a few hours each week at my daughter's school so I could see her during the day and to assist in the busy classroom. My daughter was blessed to have the same wonderful teacher for both kindergarten and grade 1.

I would sometimes come in to read to the class; or help with art, science and other projects. When the students were learning about kings, queens, and castles, I helped to make a large play castle out of cardboard and we had a king and queen luncheon. I baked and decorated a castle cake for the students, complete with a cookie and pretzel drawbridge.

Another time when the students were learning about volcanoes I made a volcano cake with candied red lava coming out of the top and red jelly lava flowing down the sides of the cake. At the base I had made cookie crumb dirt with green chocolate melts in the shape of plants. This cake accompanied the science and art units on volcanoes where the children made individual papier-mâché volcanoes and got to make them "explode" with the help of baking soda and vinegar.

I also helped make a prayer room out of cardboard that allowed the children quiet time to pray on their own. I cut out a cross and painted it for the teacher to attach to the front. There was a small table, chair, and some books about Jesus in the children's chapel. The young students knew it was a special place and would finish their work quickly and well so they could have a chance to draw close to God.

This was a creative and enriching time to be helping at the school. It was deeply satisfying and rewarding in a way the world often overlooks but they were some of my happiest times. To be amongst eager, joyful children learning, sharing, and celebrating is a special way to spend an afternoon. It can bring us back in time to when we were children filled with wonder and enthusiasm about learning and growing or give us a fresh perspective on our life in the here and now.

8

Warning

It was during this time that I learned about Saint Faustina, a Polish nun and mystic who lived from 1905-1938. She received visions of Jesus and messages from Him to share with the world. She recorded them in her diary which was published after her death. One of the messages from Jesus she was to share was one about a worldwide Warning, a global examination of conscience from Jesus. He told her, "Before I come as the Just Judge, I am coming first as the King of Mercy." I was immediately drawn to this powerful message and wanted to know more.

I began researching the history of this revelation and was drawn deep into study. Through Saint Faustina, Jesus requested the establishment of a novena (9-day prayer)—Divine Mercy novena—and a feast day—Divine Mercy Sunday—on the first Sunday after Easter. Pope John Paul II (now Saint John Paul II) promoted the Divine Mercy devotion and it spread throughout the world. Jesus promised that if a soul fulfilled the requirements of Divine Mercy Sunday that He would give them complete pardon and they could go directly to Heaven when they passed from this life with the temporal effects of their sin removed.

I wanted to go directly to Heaven. I didn't want a stopover in Purgatory, which Catholics and some other Christians believe to be a place of purification before Heaven if we are not ready to immediately enter Heaven after our death. It is found in some older Bibles but has been removed from many newer versions.

> It is therefore a holy and wholesome thought to pray for the dead, that they may be loosed from sins. (2 Maccabees 12:46)

The reality is that prayers for souls in hell are wasted because they will never get out of that eternal jail. Souls in Heaven do not need our prayers as they are in eternal joy. Souls in Purgatory do need our prayers to help them move higher up in the levels of Purgatory until they are purified and ready to enter Heaven. It is another way we can pray people into Heaven. Nothing unholy enters Heaven. We *can* attain holiness. God has provided the ways for us to become holy. Divine Mercy Sunday is a great act of His mercy in the times we are living in.

> But nothing unclean will enter it, nor anyone who practices abomination or falsehood, but only those who are written in the Lamb's book of life. (Revelation 21:27)

The worldwide Warning is expected to happen soon. There will be signs before it happens. There will be a cross in the sky and there will be light emitting from where Jesus was nailed to the cross. We must go into our homes, remain there, and pray. When the time is right, Jesus will draw all of our souls to Him for approximately twenty minutes. He will show us the state of our souls and we will receive a mini-judgement and review of our lives. He will also allow us to experience where we would go at that time based on the state of our soul, whether to Hell, Purgatory or Heaven. For those who unfortunately will experience Hell, it will be a disturbing experience. For those experiencing Purgatory, it could be very upsetting based on what level they are placed. For those ready for Heaven, they will be given a glimpse of the loving world of Heaven.

Jesus will warn each of us about different things, with some specific to our circumstances. One crucial warning for all will be *not* to take the Mark of the Beast, which more than likely will be a specific imbedded computer chip or possibly a trans-dermal computer chip tattoo in our bodies. The Mark will eventually be used to control us and will keep us from going to Heaven. It is spiritually dangerous. Avoid it at all costs, even if you are called to give up your earthly life!

> It also forced all people, great and small, rich and poor, free and slave, to receive a mark on their right hands or on their foreheads, so that they could not buy or sell unless they had the mark, which is the name of the beast or the number of its name. This calls for wisdom. Let the person who has insight calculate the number of the beast, for it is the number of a man. That number is 666. (Revelation 13:16-18)

When the Warning is over, Jesus will send our souls back to our bodies and life will resume. Only this time, there will be millions of conversions to Jesus because people are going to now believe! There are going to be approximately six weeks to help our friends and family to get ready by receiving the Sacraments of the church, especially the Sacrament of Reconciliation (Confession).

Unfortunately, there are going to be some people that will fall away again. There will be others that will not convert. Some scientists, and government leaders, will try to dismiss the Warning experience as an explainable scientific phenomenon. Beware! There will be people that will be so shocked by the state of their souls as Jesus sees them that they may die in mortal sin during the Warning. We are to pray for them ahead of time. Now is the time to get right with God so our souls are ready for the Warning!

Around the time of learning about Divine Mercy Sunday, I discovered that there was a Divine Mercy service happening in my city the Sunday after Easter. I carefully made sure to follow all the requirements of the devotion and on that special Sunday, I attended a beautiful service at one of the churches. The music was so beautiful and there was Adoration of the Blessed Sacrament (Jesus in the Eucharist) for a Holy Hour. I floated out of that church. I continued to attend this yearly event and every time I am so relieved and grateful to Jesus for His mercy.

No one knows exactly when and how all of the end times events are going to play out nor all of the interventions and strategies God will be using to save souls. One reason is because God doesn't want the enemy knowing everything. This is a Battle for Souls! There is reference to a *catching away* in the Bible or *Rapture* as some call it. God will take those who are ready to a place of protection, whether on earth or elsewhere. There is much speculation about this and no one knows for certain what will happen and when. The main thing to do is to get in a state of Grace and remain in it while we wait for God to unveil His plans. Also, we must do what we can to spread the Gospel and to let others know of Jesus' soon return. Time is truly running out so do your best to make a difference to those in your life today! Be courageous. Speak up. You may be the only one that someone hears the Good News from. God wants us to witness NOW! It is Harvest Time!

9

Prophecy

Through my research on Divine Mercy Sunday, I was learning more about other mystics and seers of the church. Some were approved and some were waiting to be approved, while others might take many years to be approved, if at all. There are hundreds of thousands (or more!) of private revelations that are truly from God that will never be approved by the church as they have never been presented for consideration. Sometimes a private revelation is for that person or loved ones only. At other times it is to be shared, but there may be obstacles in having this done. There have been cases where the mystic was proven false after a thorough investigation. The enemy can present something as the truth but upon careful examination, prayer, and discernment it is revealed to be false. There have been cases where a revelation has not been approved when it truly was from God, but there wasn't enough evidence. We must be very careful when considering messages from mystics and seers but also balance that with fair and thorough consideration of the evidence.

The church can take many years to investigate and verify alleged mystics and their private revelations. We are not required to believe or follow any private revelations, however if they are not against church teachings we can choose to follow them. For public revelations where there were many witnesses, if the church has approved it as worthy of belief, we are free to follow them.

Some people only want to follow what has already been established in the church for a long time as they have confidence and security in it. I am one of those people who is curious to know how God is revealing His truths in new ways that don't contravene church teachings but give us further insights into how Jesus is manifesting His wisdom and love in our world today.

If we quickly dismiss anything that is not in the Bible or has not yet been presented to or approved by the church yet, we might be missing beautiful ways that God is moving in these days. God is not limited and if He chooses to reveal His messages in a unique way, then we might consider being open to this and not shut it down too quickly. We could be overlooking something that could benefit us, help us to grow, and lead us closer to His heart in a new way. Certainly, it must align with Sacred Scripture and Sacred Tradition; however God has not revealed everything to us in the Bible. His love cannot be contained and limited. He is so much bigger than what has been compiled in the Bible, although yes, the Bible is the Word of God. He is the Creator and He is always creating, including through us, His creatures, and the talents, gifts, and opportunities He has given us.

> This is the disciple who is testifying to these things and has written them, and we know that his testimony is true. But there are also many other things that Jesus did; if every one of them were written down, I suppose that the world itself could not contain the books that would be written. (John 21:24-25)

There are many scriptures in the Bible regarding prophets and prophecy. Here are a few of the most relevant:

> Now there are varieties of gifts, but the same Spirit; and there are varieties of services, but the same Lord; and there are varieties of activities, but it is the same God who activates all of them in everyone. To each is given the manifestation of the Spirit for the common good. To one is given through the Spirit the utterance of wisdom, and to another the utterance of knowledge according to the same Spirit, to another faith by the same Spirit, to another gifts of healing by the one Spirit, to another the working of miracles, to another prophecy, to another the discernment of spirits, to another various kinds of tongues, to another the interpretation of tongues. All these are activated by one and the same Spirit, who allots to each one individually just as the Spirit chooses. (1 Corinthians 12:4-11)

> Do not quench the Spirit. Do not despise the words of prophets, but test everything; hold fast to what is good; (1 Thessalonians 5:19-21)

> If what a prophet proclaims in the name of the Lord does not take place or come true, that is a message the Lord has not spoken. That prophet has spoken presumptuously, so do not be alarmed. (Deuteronomy 18:22)

> But the one who prophesies speaks to people for their strengthening, encouraging and comfort. (1 Corinthians 14:3)

I think many equate prophecy with predicting a future event only. At times God has allowed this. It is recorded in the Bible. But at other times a prophet is given words to instruct, enlighten, and inspire others, and to reveal His love.

10

Revelation

As a Catholic growing up, my family would read the Children's Bible at the kitchen table while my mother finished the final preparations for supper. My father would guide us and let us take turns reading parts of the story. We had a large full-sized Bible on the coffee table in our living room and we knew to handle it with care and reverence.

I recall one day as a teenager opening this Bible to a random page which happened to be the beginning of the Book of Revelation. I began to read the first chapter. It was a bit daunting as I didn't understand what I was reading very well. I knew it was something about the end of time before Jesus returns. I was also a bit nervous as I knew this book was holy and that I was to honour it. I didn't think I was ready to read and try to understand these powerful scriptures about the end of times so I quickly closed it.

We heard much of the Bible through listening to scripture readings during Mass over the years and attending Catechism classes. But one thing that I did not experience was a true Bible study, not at our church, home or with friends. I did not know or understand much of the Bible and how to apply it to my life. That came much later in my life and I am still a Bible student.

My husband, a convert to the Catholic faith, had several Bibles, and he gave me one to use. It had a red cover which helped me to locate it easily and it stood out as a reminder to me to open, read, study, and pray with it. I would sometimes open it to random pages and read it for a short time. There was often something that I could apply to my life right away and I was always at peace reading it. I recall reading somewhere that the Bible is the *Living* Word of God, that it is *alive, active,* and *present* to us as we read it and can benefit our lives TODAY in the here and now.

For some reason, I felt called to read the Book of Revelation. Not any other chapter but that one would come to my mind. Over the course of several days, I was receiving a nudge to read this chapter. I didn't know why it was this particular book of the Bible, but it was a persistent calling day after day. One day I decided to begin reading it. I opened the Bible to the final chapter as I had done as a teenager, only this time I kept reading. I continued to read several pages each day and was finished in a few days.

What I read touched me deep in my soul, as it was a true revelation that we were living in these times, the end of the age—the End Times as many were calling them. I had been hearing, seeing, and reading of signs and indications that we were coming to the end years before Jesus returns. I felt a deep confirmation that this was true. Now that I knew, I thought I should be sharing it with others who didn't know just how close we are to the end of this era.

11

Shower of Love

With all my research into End Times prophecy, Bible verses, and related videos, blogs and articles, I was learning much more about God's plan concerning the coming events foretold so long ago. I felt an exhilaration about the possibility of living to witness some of these events. Despite this excitement, I oftentimes had an uneasiness about them and how they might impact me and my family, friends, and community as well as those in other parts of the world. It was sometimes difficult to find peace as I knew so many did not realize the times we are living in.

One day on a break, I was searching to read something about God, and at the top of the search results was a link to a website. I somehow knew that I should look at it and so I tapped the link. When I got to the website and read the introduction, I felt like God had led me here and that He wanted me to learn more about His plans. As the days and months went by I continued to read these messages, and slowly I began to understand the immense gravity of the times we are living in. I also got a sense that God wanted me to share this knowledge with others. Much of it was Biblically based but it was speaking of our current times.

I ordered a prayer book and would sometimes pray the beautiful prayers. They were filled with humility, love and mercy that spoke of the Father's heart. One of the prayers was about asking to feel the love of Jesus. I decided to pray this prayer with hopeful expectation.

A short time later I had an amazing dream. It was so clear and detailed, like a vision. In the dream, I was at my church, St. Peter's Catholic Church, with my family. It was time for Communion and so I went to the front of the church to receive the Eucharist. When I got there, I was immediately enveloped by a column of golden white shimmery light. It felt as though I was being showered with love. All around me was peace and this quiet that was far removed from what was happening in the church. I didn't want it to end. I truly felt the love of God in those special moments. After several minutes, I returned to my pew and then I realized I had missed Communion and I felt disheartened. My family had received Communion but I had not —or so I thought.

It was at this point that I woke up from the dream, and like the time I dreamt of Jesus on the beach, this dream felt so real, like I had really been there in the church. I could still feel this powerful love although awake.

After reflecting on the dream for a while, I realized that yes, I had received Communion with our Lord. I was immersed in His love. I was comforted with this knowledge and then I somehow knew this was the answer to the prayer of feeling the love of Jesus. It was so amazing that He would answer my prayer in such a beautiful way within my dreams. To be immersed in His love this way gave me a longing to return to that column of light and love.

12

Best-Laid Plans

I was continuing on with my business plan and had spent many months preparing it. During the first summer at home, I would spend the day with my daughter teaching her and taking her on outings. I would squeeze in my business plan work while she was playing, reading books on her own, or doing art. I would take her on outings and in the evening after she went to sleep I would focus on my business plan again.

I began to integrate more enriching learning activities with her into our schedule. We would work together on summer workbooks, do science activities, make crafts and enjoy interesting projects like making our own puppets and having a puppet show. We would go on nature walks, visit local tourist attractions, and have picnics. She loved it and so did I. It took extra effort but it was so worth it. She learned so much and each day was truly delightful for the both of us.

That summer I also volunteered at our church to help out with their Cat Chat program—a Catholic version of Vacation Bible School. Since I was creative, I decided to offer my services as the "crafts captain," which the leader of the program happily accepted. I was given a budget and crafts guide to purchase the supplies for the program. I found it so inspiring and fun to prepare, lead and supervise the crafts for each group of eager participants who moved from station to station during the evening program that lasted a few days. I did this for the following summer too.

I recall making angels for the children's take-home bags for the end of the program. I cut out the foam wings and the angel shaped body and glued them together on clothes pins, then added a face with a black marker. I made them at my kitchen table and was able to get into the crafting of many angels over a few evenings. When the last angel was created, I stepped back to observe the one hundred craft angels on my table—like a choir of angels. We hung our daughter's craft angel she received in our home and it was a constant reminder that we each have at least one Guardian Angel to help protect and guide us. Here is a prayer you can say to your Guardian Angel:

Angel of God

Angel of God, my guardian dear,
to whom God's love commits me here,
ever this day (or night) be at my side,
to light, to guard, to rule and guide.
Amen.

My daughter went back to school in September and I focused on the completion of my business plan. Once finished I submitted it to a local business agency for review. They were pleased with the level of detail in the plan and I was able to get some start-up funding. I was excited at the prospect of implementing my business plan. I got to work on all the initial business activities and followed the plan month by month. I did a mailout to introduce my company and services. I then followed up with email and telephone calls. But nothing was happening yet, and I realized it could take a while to break into the local market and to gain the trust of local businesses. At the same time, I was seeing another summer approaching and wondering what we were going to do regarding our daughter's care.

13

Angel Care

Around this time, I had another dream, like a vision, it was so clear. In the dream I was in a church in the space outside the sanctuary doors. All of a sudden a priest came up to me and was talking to me. I recall he said something about how they could use a childcare program there, and that it could be called Angel Daycare. I agreed with him in the dream and then he walked away and went through the doors to the sanctuary of the church. I woke up from the dream around this time and wondered about it.

At the time I was not considering any daycare service, but this dream was giving me clues as to what was coming because everything soon changed.

14

Divine Decision

A short time later, I was considering all the options for our daughter's summer care. My husband was busy with his music and I knew I had to produce some type of income generating work. If I went to a company to work again, our daughter would be back to a daycare setting and I didn't think that was the best option for her. There would also be the huge cost of a daycare program and I didn't think it was worth paying a large chunk of our income to what would be a mediocre program. After Daddy Daycare and Mom & Daughter Days, I knew we couldn't go back to regular daycare.

Then it came to me that I might be able to offer childcare services to other families. I would be able to continue being with my daughter and offer enriching programming for her as well as share it with other children, all while making money with something I truly enjoyed doing. I had a sense that this could work.

I quickly contacted St. Peter's Catholic Church to inquire about space availability. The secretary spoke with the priest and got back to me quickly, requesting that I submit a proposal. I prepared a proposal over the next couple of days. The words, ideas, plans, and goals all came together quickly. I submitted it and waited and prayed. Within a few days I was contacted by the secretary who announced that the proposal was accepted. They would provide space in the church basement in the former library for me to operate from. I was elated! She also told me it must have been the work of the Holy Spirit because at the meeting when my proposal was discussed it was approved unanimously and quickly.

Now that I was seeing the path I was to take in the near future, I thought I could continue with the implementation of the original business idea part-time in the evenings and weekends during the summer and focus on the childcare program during the day. I would return to my business full-time in the fall when my daughter returned to school. Little did I know how much time and energy would go into the planning, management, and leading of a summer day camp.

15

Sunbeams

After some research and reflection, I decided to call the summer day camp Sunbeams. I thought it was a fun, summer sort of name and that it would be appealing to children and parents alike. I quickly made some posters to put up at the church and school to see if some other parents would be interested in the program. At the same time, I was designing camp t-shirts, planning activities, acquiring special insurance, and setting up the space. It was a lot to get done in a short amount of time, but I kept at it all day and into the evenings. It was fun and energizing and gave me a joyful peace—knowing I was where I was meant to be.

With the first week beginning the final week of June, I had a small core group to begin with. There were other parents that signed up for a few days or a week or two throughout the summer. I was relieved that I didn't have a large group to begin with as then I would have needed to hire someone. Operating the summer camp with a few children was just enough for me to begin with.

16

Summer Fun

The first day and week went well. I had all the supplies and activities planned and enthusiasm and focus for what I was embarking upon. The children were friendly and open to all things fun and creative. I had a weekly schedule that helped the parents and children know what we would be doing. The program was active, imaginative, varied, educational, and inspiring.

The most important activity was our shared faith. We started the day with prayer to set the tone for the day. The children were eager to pray and would take turns offering their special intentions during prayer time. It created an atmosphere of care, generosity, and peace.

We had outdoor activities and games and sometimes free play where the children would enjoy the church grounds, which included beautiful gardens, paved paths, and a lovely grotto with statues depicting when the Virgin Mary appeared to St. Bernadette at Lourdes, France in 1858. The Virgin Mary, after several apparitions, announced that she was the Immaculate Conception, a term young Bernadette was unfamiliar with. It was later confirmed that this was the Virgin Mary, who was Full of Grace and indeed Immaculate, born without sin.

Notably, our local cathedral is called the Cathedral of the Immaculate Conception.

On the church grounds was a small cemetery where many Redemptorist missionary priests, who had served the area for over one hundred years, were buried. Nearby was a crucifixion scene with a depiction of Jesus on a white cross with statues of Mary and John. It was a holy reminder of what Jesus had done for all of us out of His great love. The children had a basic understanding of this and always respected this space.

The days were full and kept me extremely busy but I enjoyed each day of taking care of the children, teaching them new things, and watching them learn, explore, and grow.

After the children left for the day, I would clean the space and set up for the following day. On the weekends, I would prepare the schedule for the following week. I verified any special outings or activities happening in the city such as a program at the library, an art exhibit, or a music ensemble at a local venue. I checked the weather and used it as a guide for planning the outings. I had craft, art, and activity preparations to do plus administrative work, so my weekends were full.

When you are doing the work you have truly been called to do, it may take a lot of effort but it is deeply satisfying at the end of each day. I knew deep within my soul that this was God's will for me at this time in my life.

17

Creative Pursuits

I was a creative person myself so coming up with unique crafts and art projects came naturally to me. I made an underwater scene with craft paper on the wall of the Sunbeam's room and we would add our creations to it. We also made underwater scenes out of baggies filled with crafted sea creatures and sparkles so that when the children shook them they became like nautical snow globes. We made colourful clay oyster shells and I gave each child a plastic craft pearl to put in the centre of it. I was able to introduce some science on how pearls are made. Most importantly I introduced the Bible story about the Pearl of Great Price. I also had a Bible skit book and so we were able to practice and perform a skit related to this. The children loved the skits so much and I loved to see their delight in learning more about the Bible and expressing themselves so confidently and originally.

> **The Parable of the Pearl of Great Price**
> "Again, the kingdom of heaven is like a merchant seeking beautiful pearls, who, when he had found one pearl of great price, went and sold all that he had and bought it. (Matthew 13:45-46)

In my craft planning, I came across a Rosary made out of pool noodles. I thought the children would love making this and so I got the supplies at the local dollar store. After we strung the "beads," we sat on the floor and prayed with it. I then hung it up on the wall and sometimes we would take it down to pray. There were so many ways to help the children express their creativity and at the same time learn and explore different topics, including those of faith. They were enthusiastic learners, which made it a joy to teach them.

18

Let The Children

I integrated the faith into everything we did throughout the day. From morning prayers to grace before snacks and lunch, to reading Bible stories, acting out Bible skits, learning more about God, the Holy Family, the Angels, Saints, and virtues—the children naturally absorbed the teachings and I could see it gave them a deep peace to know there is a God who created, loves, and watches over them.

Sometimes I would hear a child mention they didn't go to church very much or not at all. They knew deep down that this was something important and they felt like they were missing out. I would encourage them and their parents where I could but it was the parents' decision as to what they chose to do on a Sunday morning. One thing I made sure of was that the children knew they were loved by God and that there was a place called Heaven that was going to be awesome. Also, I let them know that God has rules that He wants us to follow out of love for us as He knows what is best for us. It was a simple message but it reassured the children.

Jesus said, "Let the little children come to me, and do not hinder them, for the kingdom of heaven belongs to such as these." (Matthew 19:14)

19

Sidewalk Prophets

We would often take walks in the neighbourhood and sometimes would walk uptown via Harbour Passage—a paved walking and biking trail that had beautiful gardens, art installations, and a scenic view of the harbour. We would stop to eat our lunch somewhere along the way and then go for an afternoon visit to an historical attraction, concert in the park, art exhibit, library program, or visit to a splash pad.

The children knew many songs from their time at DMCS and we would also sing some songs in Sunbeams. Often as we were walking along the sidewalk on our outings one child would start singing a song. One after another, the other children would join in and we would have a sidewalk choir. I would listen and be lifted up with their praise as I led them down the street. Often other people walking near us would smile as they passed by us. Sometimes they would comment on the beautiful voices or clap after a song was completed. I am sure hearing the beautiful voices of young children singing praises to God stirred these strangers to contemplate matters beyond the everyday. The joy of children singing is contagious and easily spreads to those around them.

I wonder who needed to hear those children singing on those days? Who returned to their workplace with a spark of joy? Who was having a bad day that turned brighter? Who needed a boost of faith in the difficult circumstances of life? Joy broke through the mundane on those city streets. I hope the innocent and holy sounds the children shared floated across the city streets and into the souls that needed it most.

20

Beach Rocks

At least once each week I scheduled an outing to a local beach. Sometimes we walked, drove, or bussed, depending on which location we visited and how many children attended that week. All the children loved going to the beach and it was always the highlight of their week. They loved to splash in the water and dig in the sand.

One memorable day we were enjoying a sunny afternoon at one of the city beaches in Rockwood Park, in the centre of our city. I noticed it was really quiet on the beach. There was another group of children with their leaders, and a few parents with their children. All of a sudden one of the children in Sunbeams began to sing one of their favourite worship songs, then the other children joined in. They sounded so lovely, standing in the shade of one of the trees on the beach, their voices cascading out across the water.

They were giving a witness to God right there on the beach to strangers, some who may not have known Him or were distant from Him. The children sang a couple of songs and afterwards all was silent. No one clapped, no one said a word. Then about half a minute later, a woman nearby said, "Even the rocks will cry out." God was using these children and their beautiful voices as His instruments that day.

> When he came near the place where the road goes down the Mount of Olives, the whole crowd of disciples began joyfully to praise God in loud voices for all the miracles they had seen: "Blessed is the king who comes in the name of the Lord!" "Peace in heaven and glory in the highest!" Some of the Pharisees in the crowd said to Jesus, "Teacher, rebuke your disciples!" "I tell you," He replied, "if they keep quiet, the **stones will cry out**." (Luke 19:37-40)

21

Summer Memory Books

Each morning after prayers, we would work on Summer Memory Books. These were scrapbooks that the children would use daily to write a couple of sentences about their favourite memory of the previous day. They would then draw a related picture and decorate the page with stickers or other decorative elements. We would try our best to do Friday's memory at the end of that day before the children left for the weekend. On Monday mornings they would write about their weekend.

This scrapbooking helped with recall, printing, sentence structure, focus, patience, and creative expression. We also recorded the weather by using familiar icons of sun, cloud, and rain, along with the temperature, like weather reporters. This was a quiet, reflective time in which the children worked on their own. I insisted on quiet during this process and so the children learned to go inside their minds and memories to create their own unique pages.

The days of summer can become a blur of activities but with the daily recordings of some of these memories, the children could look back on their week and see more of an order to what they did while preserving some special times. What came out of these daily memory makers was a personal and beautiful keepsake. Years later I hope they will look through their scrapbooks and share them with the next generation as a legacy to their youth and Sunbeams summer days.

22

Designer Treat Bags

Every Friday afternoon I would give each child a brown bag—the kind used for brown bag lunches. They were asked to draw their favourite memory from the week on it with markers or crayons. I would include stickers for them to add to the bags if they wanted. There was never any problem with the children finishing their bags because they would become treat bags, which was a great incentive for them. They knew if the bag designs were not completed then they would not be filled. Once the children finished their designs, I would fill them with a few treats and some trinkets like bookmarks, pencils, stickers, small toys, and sometimes a faith-based item like a prayer card. They would receive their bags when they were picked up by their parents. It was a fun and helpful transition from the end of the week to the beginning of their weekend.

23

Seeking the Sacred

At least once each week, our group attended Mass at St. Peter's Catholic Church, mostly on Fridays. It was a beautiful way to end our week and the children were always well behaved and attentive. I had instilled in them the importance of the Mass and in being quiet and listening. Quieting children's voices and bodies is good training in self-control and in respect for those around you. I found they would even keep their friends in check with an occasional "shh."

One day one of the students told me after Mass that she had seen Jesus in the church. I asked her more about it and the following week, she showed me again, pointing to a huge almost human-shaped shadow to the right side of the altar. Unfortunately, it was not Jesus, but I was deeply moved by this child's innocence in believing it was. The large shadow that was cast on the wall was from the architecture and columns. I reassured her that Jesus was present in the church and although we couldn't see Him, He was with us.

24

Come Let Us Adore Him

On Tuesdays at St. Peter's Catholic Church there was Adoration followed by a special novena Mass. Often, I would take the children to Adoration for a part of the hour. It is a time of adoring Jesus, truly present in the Consecrated Host placed on the altar in a beautiful vessel called a Monstrance, which is Latin for "to show." We kneel or sit while we pray, read or keep still in silence before Him.

There are many graces Jesus gives to His faithful adorers. They may receive answers to prayers, insights into His plan for them, a prompting and leading to do something in a certain area of life, and many others. Some of these gifts we may not be aware we are receiving but one cannot be in front of the Living God and not receive something because He is a loving and merciful God and He appreciates and rewards those who take the time to visit Him in this special way.

I knew Adoration was a special time for the children too. They were quiet and peaceful for most of the time. Like during Mass, they were respectful and did their best to be still and quiet. Only God knows what He gave to each of these children during these short but reverent times in the quiet of the church and their souls. It is a mystery that I will leave in its wonder.

> 'Be still and know that I am God! I am exalted among the nations, I am exalted in the earth.' (Psalm 46:10)

25

Gifts of Friends

I received a call from a mother interested in having her children attend the program for a couple of weeks. On their start day, in walked three quiet children whose mother tongue was French but could speak English well too. They were bright, articulate and knew their faith well. They were respectful and participated fully in everything with a great attitude and joy. They were artistic and often had a unique creative twist on what they were working on.

Their mom was willing to come in once a week to offer some French lessons to the Sunbeams children. I was thrilled to add this to the program and the parents were pleased to have this language enrichment too.

This was the beginning of friendships between the mom and I, and her children and my daughter. I realized God sends those we need for friends at just the right time—like unexpected gifts. These meaningful friendships have continued to the present, nearly ten years later.

26

Goodbye to Summer

That first summer of the Sunbeams program was drawing to a close and I decided to have a closing celebration for the children. In addition to recognizing the completion of the summer program, I knew it would also help the children with the transition from summer to going back to school soon. But mostly I wanted it to be a celebration of what had happened that summer—all the learning, activities, music, beaches, art, friendships, and most importantly, drawing closer to God.

I planned a simple menu asking for each family to bring something. The parents were so supportive and willing to help. I thought of some games for the children, a craft to do, and prepared treat bags for them as take aways. It was a big celebration and the children were so filled with joy. I took lots of photos to remember this beautiful summer and the children that were entrusted to my care. My heart was full of love and gratitude for all I had been given.

27

Friday Fun

There was afterschool childcare at DMCS on Mondays through Thursdays; however there was no program on Fridays which was a half-day of school. I approached the church about this need and I once again submitted a proposal. It was quickly approved and so I embarked on a Sunbeams Friday Fun afternoon for the children who needed care, including my own daughter. It was going to be a similar program to the summer one and parents interested in this enrichment childcare program signed up their children.

I was busy during the week on an employment contract elsewhere, but the highlight of my week was attending the Friday noon Mass at St. Peter's Catholic Church, and then gathering the children who were attending the Sunbeams program and heading to the familiar brightly decorated space. I was so happy to continue with fun and creative activities and outings for the children throughout the school year.

Since there was already afterschool on the other days at DMCS, I wasn't able to offer similar services at the Sunbeams space in the church hall, which was disappointing, as I thought it would be a viable childcare option for parents with creative children. I decided to offer these services from my home and included storm days and professional development days when DMCS was closed. I cleared out a few areas in my home and made them Sunbeams spaces. We did homework, crafts, and outdoor activities. There were lots of great memories made in these shorter times and most importantly the children knew they were cared for. I was once again so grateful to help guide and care for the children placed in my childcare program.

28

Sunbeams Sequel

There was interest from parents in continuing Sunbeams the following summer. I took a look at my life to see what my options were. What I could still see was that my daughter was still in need of summer childcare, there were other parents interested in the program, I had enjoyed leading the program the summer before, and most importantly I felt deep within my heart and soul that I was meant to continue the following summer.

I submitted another proposal to the church and it was quickly approved. With no other clear options and a deep knowing in my heart, I proceeded to begin planning, organizing, and promoting the program for the second year. There were some returning children as well as a few new ones. Some came for the whole summer, others for a week or two.

I was beginning a new journey with this new summer, some new children, new activities and projects, and the weeks ahead unknown. Confident with the previous summer's experience to carry me forward, I knew all would be well and that the days ahead would unfold as they should: one hour at a time.

29

Holy Ground

One of the new children with us this second summer was an energetic, curious, fun-loving, and athletic boy. He was an extremely fast runner and he was an independent and original thinker. He was also exceptionally good at math as I would include some morning math and other subject activities and worksheets to help with the prevention of summer *brain drain*. When the children returned to school they would hopefully find adjusting to a desk and schoolwork a little easier. He always finished his math sheets early and they were usually all correct or occasionally with very minimal errors. He was a bit competitive which would certainly help in sports. Sometimes I had to remind him to wait his turn or wait patiently in line.

On rainy days or really hot weather or as a change of space, we would often spend time in the church hall around the corner from the main childcare room we used. It was a huge space used for church meals, wedding receptions, meetings, and other events. I was so grateful to be able to use the extra space when needed for the children. It was great for running around in, playing games or other activities for the children to expend some of their energy.

On one particular rainy day, we had finished our morning prayers and completed our Summer Memory Scrapbooks, and it was time for some activities. I announced to the children that we were going to spend some time in the church hall because it was raining. I asked the children to line up and we proceeded to the church hall space. There were a few stairs to go down and as we were making our way, the racer of the children ran ahead and got to the church hall before us. He then ran back to meet me as we were entering the main space. He had a surprised look on his face and he announced to me, "Mrs. Kipping, I think I just saw an angel." He looked so serious and honest when he told me that I thought he *had* seen someone.

I then began to ask him questions about who or what he had seen. He proceeded to give me a detailed description of a man wearing a white tunic, with a gold belt. He had curly blond hair to his shoulders. The boy then proceeded to tell me that the angel was kneeling and looking at the framed painting on the wall. This was a real painting that hung on one of the walls in the church hall. It was a painting of Jesus in the Last Supper.

Before I could comprehend what had just happened, I started hearing some of the other children singing. They had removed their shoes and were singing one of the beautiful songs they had learned from their school. I remained silent for a while listening to them, realizing something special was happening. I then asked the children why they had removed their shoes. They replied, "Because we are standing on Holy Ground." I was amazed that we were in the presence of a miracle—that something so heavenly and holy was happening in our midst.

I shared what happened with the mom of the boy and let the other parents know that something special had happened that day and that they could ask their children about it. It was a beautiful gift given to that boy, and that we got to share in it was a great honour. I won't know this side of Heaven all that it means but it raised our hearts and minds to God that day and is a cherished memory of my Sunbeams program that summer.

30

Helping Hands

The Sunbeams program had many parents and friends offering a helping hand. It was its own little community of love and light, and every act of giving helped to make the program more enriching for the children, gave me support, and rippled out to others in the community. There were many and here are only a few examples of our dear supporters:

My friend continued to offer her weekly conversational French program for the children which we all so appreciated. She made it fun and engaging and the children enjoyed putting their primarily second language into practice.

One of the moms lent the group a colourful tube-shaped play structure for the children to enjoy on rainy days. They would take turns lining up and crawling through the structure. They loved it so much and it kept them active, occupied, and having fun together.

Another mom lent the group character development cards with a description of a virtue and questions and suggestions for discussion with the children. I incorporated them into our prayer time and it certainly helped them to learn more about and grow in many virtues.

A lovely older lady I knew from the school and church circles, offered to come in to volunteer with the children. She was such a kind and gentle soul and had previously worked with some of the children at the school. I was honoured to have her spend some time with us. She came in weekly and did some gardening with the children. I brought in some gardening supplies and she brought in some beautiful flowers. We potted some flowers with the children that they could take home. They enjoyed getting their hands dirty and connecting with nature. They were so happy to have their own special gift to bring home to their mothers. Another week, the children learned how to press flowers by placing them into thick books. Our lovely friend came back the following week and we used the pressed flowers to make homemade note cards and bookmarks. She was so patient, loving, and generous with the children. I have always remembered her with a grateful heart.

My husband offered to do a drum workshop with the children. Leading up to it, I collected large plastic containers about two feet tall, with lids. I cut out thick paper to wrap around the drum and for the cover. The children then designed their own drum panel and lid, painted them, and I attached them to the plastic base and cover. They were thrilled to have their very own designer drums! We decided to hold the workshop outside in a circle. My husband demonstrated different drumming techniques, invited the children to listen and repeat the drum rhythms, then finished with a drumming performance. The children loved to hear the vibrant beat of the djembe and the lively rhythms. Their attentiveness and wide grins revealed they were enjoying their time together. At the end everyone joined in for one big drum circle of freestyle drumming, including me. It was a fun, energizing, and educational workshop. The drum is truly a universal instrument and resonates with most people, including children. It echoes the heartbeat of each of us, of the earth, the universe and beyond. I sometimes imagine my husband playing the drum in the great worship in Heaven...making a joyful noise to the Lord!

31

Rugged Cross

I began to include visits to Adoration at the Cathedral of the Immaculate Conception, the Mother Church, when our group was uptown for an activity. Sometimes it was only a quick stop in. Other times a little longer. Sometimes the children would begin singing spontaneously together. Most of the adorers were delighted to listen. The children would get up close to the Blessed Sacrament on the altar and kneel. Jesus loves the little children and enjoys having them in His presence.

On one of these visits, the children were quiet and adoring Jesus in their own special way as innocent children know how to do. These are personal encounters with Jesus in the Blessed Sacrament on the altar. I allowed King Jesus to have His special time with them. I remained silent. In the quiet, miracles can happen.

Right after one of these visits, one of the children, who had lost her father a couple of years before, began to share something remarkable with me about that day's Adoration. I had not known this little girl's father but I did recall seeing him once at Mass at St. Peter's Catholic Church shortly before he died. I had noted his skin was ruddy and I could tell he was not well. I was moved to pray for him and his family, knowing he was getting ready to leave this earth. A subsequent conversation with the little girl's mother at the church revealed he was not well and confirmed he did not have long to live. It was a sad time for the little girl to lose her daddy at such a young and tender age. But God's ways are higher than ours and through all the suffering, Jesus was able to receive another beloved soul into His kingdom.

On this particular day of Adoration, the little girl told me that during Adoration, Jesus took her hand and led her to Heaven to meet her dad! The important detail that she added was that the skin on his face was smooth. She remembered while he was on the earth that his face was red and rough, but now in Heaven it was healed. I responded that it was amazing that Jesus took her to see her dad. I reminded her that her dad was watching from Heaven and loved her very much and that someday in the future she would go to Heaven and be with him always. I didn't ask anymore questions about her encounter because I thought it was something special between her and her dad and I would leave it be.

When her mother picked her up a bit later, I eagerly shared what had happened. She mentioned that the medication her husband had been taking made his skin red. She did not say too much but pondered what I had shared. I hope this gift gave her peace of mind and heart knowing her husband was now with the Lord forever, and that her daughter was accompanied by Jesus to visit him. I am sure it would have been a gift for her dad too.

32

Sunbeams Service

I discussed with the children about doing a Sunbeams service project. We decided on a lemonade stand with funds raised going to one of the city's food banks. The children were enthusiastic about the project, its planning and the actual lemonade stand. They made posters that we put up in the neighbourhood and flyers they shared with family and friends.

On the day of the lemonade sale we decorated the tables outside, prepared the lemonade, and waited with great expectation. Some people, including parents, stopped by as well as others from the community and those passing by. The children were very friendly and would call to potential customers walking across the church grounds, inviting them to buy a glass of lemonade for a good cause. One of the people walking by shared that he didn't have any money at the time. It was such a hot day and we decided to show some mercy by giving the man a free glass of refreshing lemonade. I know that glass of cold lemonade went farther than quenching the man's thirst that hot summer day. The children were beaming with joy at being able to share a glass of their lemonade with someone in need. Children have an innocent sense of justice and fairness and in their simplicity is found a beautiful love for others and their often-unspoken needs.

33

Friday Finale

Living in the Spirit of God came so naturally to the children and so I wanted them to be given as many opportunities to be close to Jesus as possible. I continued to include Mass on Fridays as a regular part of the schedule. The children knew it was a special time and were always filled with such joy and peace. It was a beautiful way to end the week.

After lunch and the making of the designer treat bags, the children would once again enjoy the beautiful church grounds. There was plenty of green space for the children to run around in and a peaceful setting to enjoy. All around us were holy reminders: the grotto, the crucifixion, the cemetery headstones of dedicated servants of Christ, the loving school and welcoming church with its cross of hope.

A new addition for this summer was a sprinkler for the children to run through on hot days, as well as a small inflatable pool. We always had outdoor toys and plenty of chalk which kept the children busy. One of their favourite things to do was to blow the bubbles with the various shapes and sizes of wands, and to chase and break the bubbles. Sunny Friday afternoons were delightful for the children as well as for me who got to glimpse the Father's joy through His children.

34

Dreams & Visions

Starting around this time, I began to have many dream visions that were powerful and inspiring. These were not regular dreams. They had incredible detail, clarity, and spiritual significance that I believe were given to me by God.

This intense period of dreams continued for a couple of years. I always had an interesting one to share with a close family member or a trusted friend. The dreams included being given a ring from Jesus; being dressed in a beautiful white dress, looking young and beautiful as though a bride; seeing Jesus humbly serving at the heavenly banquet; Jesus dressed in a white tunic with sandals on His feet; running out of my home saying Jesus was here and being lifted up off the ground by a powerful force; watching the New Jerusalem coming down from Heaven; and seeing some of what God has prepared for me in Heaven.

There are many details to these dreams and many more dreams I had that are not listed. I know they were Heaven inspired and experiencing them myself has deepened my faith and encouraged me to keep moving forward with hope. But because they are so incredibly detailed and spectacular, they are too good to keep to myself and so on occasion I have felt inspired to share a few dreams with others. I think the dreams have been gifted to me to help encourage others in their walk too as there has never been one person who seemed sceptical of what I shared about my dreams. If anything, they were amazed and grateful to hear what I had to share. They always left uplifted and hopeful of something beyond this passing world.

> And I saw the holy city, the new Jerusalem, coming down out of heaven from God, prepared as a bride adorned for her husband. (Revelation 21:2)

35

Opening My Eyes

Something that God had begun to make me more aware of a few years before were the homeless and struggling in our city. For so many years, really for most of my life up until this point, I would avoid anyone that seemed like they might be homeless. I was uncomfortable around them and a little nervous, never knowing what to expect or what to say. I also admit that I didn't have much empathy for them, thinking they got themselves into their predicament through too much drinking or drugs or both. I also realize now that I looked down on them as not being good enough, thinking they were not willing to make much effort in improving their circumstances.

I had so much to learn and so God began to teach me. I began to notice the homeless people hidden in plain sight. I would sometimes say *hello* as I quickly dropped a few coins in their cup as I passed by, keeping my distance. Sometimes I would mimic what others did, like getting an extra coffee and giving it to them. But it was usually from a place of detachment and doing my duty.

The Great Teacher is patient and so He will slowly introduce people and situations to test us or teach us. I would sometimes give one of my prayer cards to one of the street people, like a spiritual coffee as I walked by. Sometimes I would give them both a real coffee and a prayer card. They were mostly grateful to receive both, but I do recall one person refusing to take the prayer card as he adamantly professed his unbelief. He was so hardened by the street life that he could not even consider there was something or someone beyond the daily struggles. I was moved to pray for him and I hope he is doing better.

I was beginning to notice that underneath the often-dirty hands and clothes, there was a sadness, and even a hopelessness that was palpable. Again, God was training me to look deeper into the humanity of these people. I began to wonder about them and what events and circumstances had led them to this point of begging for help on the side of the road.

I began to research and learn about homelessness and the many factors that can lead someone to become without a home. Losing a job, relationship and family breakdowns, abuse in its many forms, addictions, trauma, and mental health issues were some of the complex and painful reasons for homelessness.

Sometimes I would share a snack I had with a hungry person. At other times I would buy them a sandwich from a coffee shop. I recall seeing someone had actually made a homeless person a homemade lunch and had brought the meal to him right in the pan. I observed he sat with the person and talked with him, like you would talk to a friend. I was deeply moved by this encounter and it stirred me to try to connect more with those I would meet on the side of our city's streets.

It would take many more months until I would actually stop and really talk with someone who was struggling, but when I did I was often given beautiful gifts of insight, compassion, and understanding. God was helping me to grow to see these people the way He does. After all, they are His beloved children too and He does not have favourites.

I especially felt a calling to pray for the homeless and struggling I met. Sometimes I would give them a prayer card, a coffee, a small gift card, a snack or sandwich, but I realized that feeding their stomachs or passing them a prayer card was not enough. They needed to hear a message of hope and of love. I began to speak to them what I felt led to share and sometimes would ask if they would like me to pray with them. Most of the time, it was a yes. I found so many of these struggling people were open to having someone pray with them. This was because they had nothing left to lose but something to gain. Even a small improvement in their situation would be welcomed. In this moment of trust they reached out with a glimmer of hope in a Higher Power.

With the Sunbeams program I instilled the importance of valuing everyone and that we are all equal in God's eyes as He made and loves us all. The children easily understood this and we would sometimes pray for the homeless people during morning prayers.

Sometimes when the children were walking with me uptown to or from an activity we would come across a homeless person. I was careful not to involve the children too much; however I would often point out a person who I thought might not have a place to live and we would pray for them a distance away.

There was one time when one of the children saw a homeless person sitting on the sidewalk and he must have whispered it to the other children as they all came up to me quietly and urgently asking if I had any change to give. They all were so concerned about this man without a home and eager to do their small part to make it better. I quickly took out some change and gave it to them thinking this was an important lesson in compassion for others, especially the most vulnerable. The children all hurried to drop the coins into the man's coffee cup and most importantly they smiled at him and said *hello*. It was truly better to give than to receive that day as the children were beaming and so was the homeless man. I was too!

For I was hungry and you gave me something to eat, I was thirsty and you gave me something to drink, I was a stranger and you invited me in, (Matthew 25:35)

36

Summer Sunset

The second summer of Sunbeams drew to a close. We celebrated with another closing party in the church hall. Delicious food brought by the parents, music, games, laughter, and treat bags all made for a special ending of our summer journey. Another beautiful summer filled with great memories would live on in our hearts, minds, and souls.

As my daughter and I walked home after the last child left and clean up was completed, I gazed at the beautiful golden sunset. The sun was setting on the wonderful day we had experienced, and on another Sunbeams summer. I felt deep contentment and peace, knowing I had completed what I was called to do.

37

Work from Home

I once again offered my childcare services from my home. It was convenient and comfortable to have my home as the base. The childcare program I offered was mostly after-school as well as Friday afternoons, snow days, professional development days for the teachers, and some holidays if needed. Sometimes I also offered extended hours into the evening and would make supper for the children who stayed. I tried to make it a home away from home for the children with a mix of learning, creative pursuits, homework, fresh air, and fitness.

There was one little girl in particular who I took care of on a regular basis. She became like a little sister to my daughter and they both got along well. They both enjoyed much of the same things, including playing with dolls, imaginative play, music, reading, and art. There were many happy times and memories made over the next few years.

There were other children I took care of too who always had something unique to add to the group. These were always fun times with creative pursuits and friendships that blossomed.

38

Foyer Fear

I began to have an inner prompting to do more in regard to sharing the Good News of Jesus with others. What kept coming to me was that the Lord wanted me to put prayer cards in my neighbours' mailboxes. Not wanting to appear as though I was snooping in mailboxes I tried to discount the thoughts. But they kept coming back to me, like recurring thoughts tend to do, until something is acted upon. I continued to dismiss the thoughts but they would not go away. They weren't intrusive or obsessive thoughts, but gentle reminders.

As I thought more about my uncomfortableness in doing this task I began to realize that there was also a bit of pride in the mix as I did not want my neighbours to see me doing this; some anxiety as I was concerned about what I might say if asked; and also some fear as I wondered what they might say or do if they saw me opening mailboxes. But each day that I tried to ignore the promptings, they only got stronger.

Finally one day I decided that I would do what I thought I was being asked to do. I printed, cut, and folded a stack of prayer cards. I laced up my sneakers, put on my jacket and looked out my front door window up and down the street. There were a lot of houses on my street, and a lot of mailboxes. My palms were sweaty and my heart was beating faster than usual as I was nervous about what I was about to do.

But first I wanted to see if I could get some kind of confirmation that this was what the Lord was expecting of me. So I thought I would open my Bible to a random spot and begin reading and see if I received any insights. As I began to read the Bible passages while seated in my foyer, I relaxed a bit. I wasn't sure how far I intended to read but I was only a couple of minutes in when I came across one of the scriptures that I had included on my prayer card printouts to put in the mailboxes. It was either coincidence or confirmation, but I went with the latter.

I took a deep breath, prayed a few prayers, and walked out my front door as though a soldier in the Lord's army with my marching orders—albeit a reluctant one. It was a sunny fall day when I overcame my fear about what others thought and began to truly be more concerned about what God thought about me and my service to Him.

As I went along placing the prayers in mailboxes, the nervousness seemed to subside. I went up and down the street quickly placing the prayers in mailboxes or mail slots. Amazingly I did not encounter one person while I did this. It was as though this was training day and Jesus was keeping the potential doubters, mockers, and aggressors away—at least for today. I quickly completed my call of duty and returned home thinking I had fulfilled my role in the Great Commission and that I would now be left alone to pursue other interests. I was wrong, very wrong, as this was only the beginning.

The Great Commission

Then the eleven disciples went to Galilee, to the mountain where Jesus had told them to go. When they saw him, they worshiped him; but some doubted. Then Jesus came to them and said, "All authority in heaven and on earth has been given to me. Therefore go and make disciples of all nations, baptizing them in the name of the Father and of the Son and of the Holy Spirit, and teaching them to obey everything I have commanded you. And surely I am with you always, to the very end of the age." (Matthew 28:16-20)

39

Little Flowers

Earlier in the same year, during a church brunch, I had been approached by a parent wondering if I might be interested in helping to lead a program for girls called "Little Flowers." She told me I had come to mind as someone she thought could help. I didn't know her very well but she seemed very interested in the program. She explained a little bit about it and proposed that we meet over the summer to discuss.

We set a meeting time and when I saw some of the program materials that a friend had given her, I was immediately interested. The program's patron saint was St. Thérèse of Lisieux, who had spent her life doing "small things with great love." This saint also promised that she would "let fall a shower of roses" once she got to Heaven. There have been many miracles attributed to St. Thérèse's intercession, with roses often appearing in confirmation of prayers answered.

The Little Flowers program had workbooks with weekly teachings on various saints and the virtues they were known for. A different flower applying to each saint was also discussed. There was also a beautiful colouring sheet, a unique craft that connected with the teachings and a themed snack to finish with.

There was also a uniform for each girl to wear while attending the program each week that consisted of a light pink shirt, light blue bandana for their hair, and a light blue sash for sewing on badges the girls would earn by fulfilling the requirements for each week.

I did some research and thought it would be a lovely program for my daughter, along with the other girls that would join. We submitted a proposal to the church and were given the church hall to use for the program, which would start later in the year. We were both excited about helping the girls grow in virtues and faith through this wonderful program.

We set a fee for the program that included the uniform, workbooks, badges, crafts, and snacks. I designed a flyer and we posted and promoted it through the school and church. Within a couple of weeks the program had several girls registered. We had the parents fill out the registration forms and then we ordered the supplies.

The program started with an enthusiastic group of girls. I would lead the group activities and teachings based on the Leader's Manual, followed by a craft. My program partner would prepare the snacks, set up and help clean and tidy up afterwards. We sang songs, prayed, crafted, and enjoyed snacks that tied in with the teachings. It worked out well and the weeks went along quickly as the girls grew in their knowledge and understanding of each saint and their outstanding virtues. It was a wonderful program to lead and I enjoyed seeing the girls accomplish their goals to receive badges.

When the program was nearing completion, one of the parents offered to host a closing Mother and Daughter Tea and Luncheon. I was deeply touched by her generous hospitality and in hosting at her lovely home. It would be the finishing touch to the learning and growth in virtue the girls had experienced over the past several months.

I prepared invitations for each girl to give to their mothers with all the details. We planned a luncheon menu and each mother and daughter contributed to the food table. The hostess was gracious to her guests with her beautiful smile and welcoming heart and home. She and her daughter had decorated the long dining room table with beautiful tableware, including a classic tea set.

The girls got dressed up in their best dresses and white gloves for the special occasion. The mothers were dressed up as well and we took some lovely photos together. It was a delightful afternoon and a lesson in refinement for the small yet special guests—beautiful little flowers indeed!

> "You know well enough that Our Lord does not look so much at the greatness of our actions, nor even at their difficulty, but at the love with which we do them." (St. Thérèse of Lisieux)

40

Queen of Peace

I had noted an ongoing announcement in our church's bulletin about a Queen of Peace Prayer Group that happened weekly. I usually scanned it as I was reading the other posts, but eventually I became curious about it and thought I might like to attend. I was unable to go in the early years as the prayer group went later in the evening and my daughter was at the age where she needed my presence more. As she got a bit older, I decided that it was time to visit the prayer group and see what it was all about. Making sure my husband would be home, I got our daughter to sleep early and made my way to the prayer group.

It was a welcoming group and somehow even though it was my first time attending it felt like home to me. There was beautiful singing, often accompanied by guitar. There were prayers, and requests for prayers for others. Bible scriptures would be read, the Rosary prayed, and often someone would be given a word from the Lord to share. Sometimes someone would share a vision or image they had.

What I found so amazing was when everyone was singing together, I would hear some strange yet comforting sounds from some of the people. I learned that the people were "speaking in tongues" which was a gift from the Holy Spirit. There were times when the singing would stop and there was a chorus of people speaking in tongues. It sounded as heavenly as if they were angels singing, and I felt such peace. It was all new to me as I had never been exposed to a prayer group before, even when growing up in the church. But I liked it and wanted to continue attending.

My husband wasn't always available to be home on the evening that I had the prayer group. As our daughter was getting older and able to stay up a little later, I thought I would try taking her along. A friend from school and her mother would attend and eventually our daughters and sometimes a few other children would join. They loved the singing especially as they knew many of the praise songs from their school.

The children were so filled with joy when singing the songs and you could tell the presence of the Lord was with them. Afterwards they would often go to the side table to colour or draw as I had set up a craft table for them. I recall one evening they made a lot of small notes with images and decorations on them with reminders of how much God loves us and handed them out to all in attendance. The recipients were deeply touched by this sweet gesture, no doubt one that had been guided by the Holy Spirit.

Initially we would leave a bit earlier so my daughter would have a good night's sleep. As she got older, we would often stay for the whole time and enjoy some snacks and fellowship afterwards. It filled us both with energy, joy and love that carried us through the week.

I eventually signed up for a "Life in The Spirit" seminar that the prayer group was hosting. It was through this group that I had confirmed that I had received the Baptism of the Holy Spirit over a decade before. This time, as I prayed asking for another outpouring of the Holy Spirit, I also asked for the Gift of Tongues. Perhaps I already had been given it and didn't know it, but this time I specifically requested it.

The leaders helped to guide me in how to get started speaking in tongues. Initially it felt weird and awkward but as I continued at home I began to make more sounds with my prayer language. What was peculiar at first was that it seemed like I could only do this on one side of my mouth. I am not sure why, but it was a couple of years before I could speak in tongues fully with my whole tongue and mouth.

> While Peter was still speaking these words, the Holy Spirit came on all who heard the message. The circumcised believers who had come with Peter were astonished that the gift of the Holy Spirit had been poured out even on Gentiles. For they heard them speaking in tongues and praising God. (Acts 10:44-46)

I began to speak in tongues during the prayer group. Once, I had a vision of huge columns and glimpsed the beautiful interior of a building—like a temple. I also heard an interior phrase spoken, "The Third Heaven." The words had come from within my mind but seemed to have been spoken to me. I didn't know what the "Third Heaven" was. Over the next few days I did some research and came to find out that the Third Heaven is written about in the Bible and is the abode of God. I believe my being, through worship, was caught up to Heaven for a very short time.

> I know a man in Christ who fourteen years ago was caught up to the third heaven. Whether it was in the body or out of the body I do not know—God knows. And I know that this man—whether in the body or apart from the body I do not know, but God knows— was caught up to paradise and heard inexpressible things, things that no one is permitted to tell. (2 Corinthians 12:2-4)

I was initially hesitant about speaking in tongues but eventually overcame my uneasiness by practicing and experiencing the power of it. I know a lot of other people are uncomfortable regarding it but it is written about in the Bible and many people use their special prayer language to praise God. I also learned that one can fight in the Spirit with it. Oftentimes I would begin praying and then move into spiritually battling with my prayer language for difficult situations, relationships, and events where I could sense the enemy—and still do to this day. Speaking in tongues is spiritually powerful. I invite you to discover your special prayer language. There are resources that can help get you started whether at your church, in print or online. Pray about it first and ask the Lord to lead you to helpful resources and the right people to guide you.

41

Quick Switch

I was teaching Catechism at St. Peter's Catholic Church for several years. It had begun when I was taking my younger son to Catechism when he was with me every second weekend. We would walk to the church early Sunday morning along with my young daughter. My daughter and I would wait for my son and then we would attend Mass, meeting my husband there. When my daughter became old enough to join a class, I would then read or pray in the church hall while I waited for them.

After several years of living with me, my son was now based at his dad's due to a decision we agreed upon. My son was taking French Immersion and since his dad was French, he was able to help him more with his French lessons and homework. It was a sacrifice I made for him to succeed at school and so he would have a good knowledge of both languages. He did well in school and eventually he moved to a large French city where he continued his education and enjoyed the language and culture. It was still not easy and I missed him and didn't see him as much as I would have liked, but sometimes these difficult choices and letting go are meant for growth for everyone.

After a few weeks of waiting during the Catechism class, I thought I could help out since I was there anyway. I had taught Catechism when I was a teenager at my childhood church and had enjoyed it. I offered to assist a teacher one week and then quickly I was invited to have my own class as they were short a teacher. I stepped up to it and led classes for several years.

Towards the end I was beginning to sense that I was not long to continue in this role. I began to have less enthusiasm for being a Catechism teacher but was trying to continue as best I could. Then one Sunday I just could not do it anymore. The pull to something else was so strong that I actually called the leader's home that morning and informed her husband I would not be able to continue. I knew there was another woman who was helping out that could fill my role. When I hung up the phone I felt such relief but didn't quite understand it.

I dropped off my children for their Catechism class but I continued on my way. I took a drive through part of the city. I then went through a drive-through coffee shop and ordered a breakfast sandwich and juice as somehow I felt like I was meant to give this to someone. It was like I was being led by some powerful force and so I followed the promptings.

The next thing I recall I was now out of the car and talking to two strangers who I sensed were in need. I offered them the sandwich and juice, suggesting they could share it. They gladly accepted and began eating. While they ate, I made some small talk and included some references to God. I found out they were a father and son. They shared some sad stories from their past and I felt deep compassion for them both.

During the conversation I felt like I should give them one of my prayer cards that I had made. The older man had a problem with his vision and could not read and so I asked him if I could pray the prayer aloud with him and his son. He humbly agreed and so I nervously spoke the prayer with them both and he listened with his heart, mind and soul and spoke the "Amen" aloud with me at the end. I then wished them both a good day, got in my car and drove away. It was the beginning of many encounters the Lord would open up for me to share the Good News.

I ran into the adult son from this meeting a couple of years later. I asked about his dad and he told me his father had died. I asked how long ago and he replied with the month and the year. I expressed my sympathy and comforted him as best I could with this sad reminder of his loss. Later after thinking about the conversation and the timeframe, I realized his father's death had occurred within a few months after our encounter on the side of the road. That was more than likely why I felt such an urgency to move in a different direction that Sunday morning. I won't know this side of Heaven and that's alright with me, as we aren't meant to know everything here. But if I was able to assist someone in drawing close to Christ, I am forever grateful that I was of service to Him.

42

Voice of God

With drawing closer to God, I began to realize how time was short—not only in one's life but in the collective humanity currently living on earth. Yes, as the Bible says no one knows the day or the hour. But it also says that we can know the season—not the literal seasons of spring, summer, winter or fall, but times and events that point to the soon return of Jesus.

I would do my best to make time for prayer each day. Some days were better than others depending on the competing duties, and oftentimes, distractions. On the days that I really made time for dedicated prayer time with God, I was often given insights that were helpful in my daily life as well as in my life as a whole.

Sometimes when I was praying I would feel a deep sadness for the lost souls. Without despairing, an urgency to pray for them would well up inside me and soon my kitchen became a battlefield as I went into intense spiritual battle for the souls of family, relatives, friends, neighbours and even strangers. These were powerful times and I know the enemy did not like it. But I felt a deep call to do this, harkening back to the elderly lady at the church quietly informing me that I can *pray others into Heaven*. It became a cornerstone of my prayer time and remains as such to this day.

I recall on one particular morning while in prayer that the presence of God was so powerful in my kitchen that it moved me to tears. I was kneeling and praying for the lost and God was there with me. I moved to the other side of the kitchen to sit and continued praying. All of a sudden I clearly heard in my spirit, "Take the Gospel to the Street." It was a simple yet powerful sentence, spoken with authority. It was what I later learned to be an auditory word from God, also known as a locution. I knew it did not come from me. It was a voice outside of me, yet felt and heard interiorly, deep in my soul. It was the confirmation that I needed to hear. I had been doing some informal street evangelizing as I felt like that was the direction I was being led to. To hear these words spoken to me gave me peace and a deep knowing that I was meant to continue in this calling.

At another time in prayer I heard the word "Pray!" It was spoken with intensity and had an urgency about it. It was clear to me that God wanted and needed my prayers and that I needed to ramp up my prayer time. It is amazing that God allows us to help Him in the redemption of His beautiful souls. I will never truly know this side of Heaven how I have helped Him but I am honoured to be one of His instruments in leading others to Jesus, the Redeemer of the World.

Of special note, on another day while praying I heard a word spoken to me: "Endure." I was not afraid to hear these locutions as I had come to realize they were a gift given to guide and protect me. "Endure" is spoken of in the Bible. That one simple word packs a lot of meaning concerning my life and its circumstances. It was also a prophetic word from God to help me in the coming months and years with all that would transpire in my life and in the world. It is also a word for everyone as we are all called to endure despite the hardships we may find in our lives. Whenever I have had setbacks, I find recalling the day I received this word has helped strengthen me. God wants us all to take up our cross and follow Him. He will walk with us and help us to carry our cross.

> But the one who endures to the end will be saved.
> (Matthew 24:13)

43

Pet Petition

My daughter had wanted a pet for a long time. Over the years she would hear of some of her classmates' getting pets and sometimes they would be brought to school for a visit. She would be so excited to meet the new creature and would delight in sharing the details with me after school. But sometimes she would look a bit sad and would share that she would like to have a pet of her own. I would reassure her that sometime in the future she would have her very own pet.

While waiting for her real pet, she would find substitutes on walks home from school. There was the slug who, for a couple of days, lived in a decorated shoebox that she filled with grasses, rocks, and a container of water. Next came the water bug that she kept in a baggie of water overnight. There was an inchworm too but it stayed outside. She would learn about her nature pets and even give them a name. She didn't want to let them go but we would let her know they were just visiting us and that their real home was in nature. The slug returned to a field nearby; the water bug we released in a pond in our city park. There were many tears as our daughter said goodbye to the little creatures that she so desperately tried to make into pets. My husband and I realized that it was really important for our daughter to get her own real pet, and soon. She had a big heart and wanted her own pet to love and care for.

I made a chart with my daughter and we listed all the items that a cat would need, along with their costs. We included the basics plus vet visits and emergency costs. The total start-up costs and ongoing food and litter, though not huge monthly costs, were enough that I was still concerned about always having enough, in our already tight budget, for a cat. Then we listed all the duties and responsibilities involved with taking care of a cat. I wanted my daughter to realize that getting a pet was a big responsibility and a long-term commitment. She was enthusiastic about it and agreed that she would always take care of her cat.

Often when we were praying our nighttime prayers, my daughter would include a request for a pet, specifically a cat. It was sweet to hear her daily prayer. Her persistence was always with an innocent trust that her prayer would be heard and hope that it would be answered favourably someday.

I recall finding a prayer card having a special prayer asking for St. Thérèse of Lisieux's intercession. With faith and hope, I decided to pray it, with the intention that God would provide the perfect cat for my daughter, in His perfect time. I didn't tell my daughter about this prayer I had prayed on her behalf. It was a quiet, private prayer from a mother's heart to the heart of the Father.

It wasn't long after this prayer that my husband came home after being out one Tuesday morning in October and told me that an acquaintance of his who lived a couple of blocks away had two cats. One was originally his mother's and he had been given it due to her having a couple of dogs that this cat didn't get along with. This man also had another cat, and when he adopted the second from his mother, the two cats didn't get along. He then got very sick and couldn't take care of them both. The first cat was more of an outdoor cat who came and went, so he was trying to find a home for the second cat. I needed no convincing and told my husband I was fine with us adopting the cat. Through all these years of my daughter pining for a cat, I always thought we would adopt a kitten but now we were about to adopt an adult cat—a young adult cat, about 13 months old.

The next morning my husband went out early and a couple of hours later he arrived home with a cat in a pet carrier. I knew the cat might be available soon, within the week, but I didn't realize it would be the next day. Often the timing of something might be different from our expectations but being flexible and open to life's surprises can bring beautiful experiences, people and even cats into our lives.

We left the cat in the carrier while my husband unloaded all the supplies. The neighbour had generously given us all we needed to get started taking care of our new cat: litter box, litter, cat food, food dishes, cat brush, collar, cat scratch pad, and toys. I could hardly believe it. Not only did we get a lovely cat for free but all the supplies and food to keep us going for many months. It was a wonderful Wednesday and I was feeling so grateful for all that had been delivered to our home, especially this sweet, little creature.

The cat was meowing and so we decided to open the pet carrier door and see what she would do. She slowly came out and nervously looked around. She had such a look of fear in her eyes that my heart went out to her. She had large jade green eyes, and above them the distinct tabby *M* marking. She was a mix of tabby and calico with dark stripes on grey as well as blotches of black, orange, and white. She was beautiful, delicate, timid, and she was now ours.

She was in unfamiliar surroundings with two strangers, not knowing what to do nor where to go. She took a few steps down the hall. I squatted and put my hand out. She came and sniffed it and I heard a little purr. I cautiously patted her and spoke softly to her, telling her this was her new home and we were going to take good care of her. She walked to the end of the hall and went up the stairs to the second level to find a safe space to hide for a few hours.

My husband told me her name was Rosemary. I spoke her name aloud and then I said, "Rosie." Somehow I knew her name was going to be Rosie. A new home, and a slightly new name. Rosie it was. I thought about the St. Thérèse prayer and how often people receive a sign that their prayer has been answered by receiving a rose in some form. Hmmm. Rosemary...Rosie. Yes, my prayer and my daughter's many prayers over the years had been answered. God provided all the supplies too. Oftentimes, when God answers prayers, the events can happen quickly and over a short time. Within 24 hours of learning about this cat needing a new home, she was now ours.

My daughter was in school and I knew she was going to be thrilled to meet her new pet. It was such an amazing answer to prayer and I wanted her to realize the importance of prayer and *persistent* prayer. Also, I wanted her to know that God had heard her prayers. I also wanted her to understand this was the beginning of a long-term commitment for the duration of the cat's life, come what may.

I was inspired to write a letter to my daughter from the perspective of Rosie. It was written in the first person as though Rosie was speaking to my daughter. Rosie "shared" a bit about her past, the circumstances of her adoption, and looking for her fur-ever home. Also, Rosie mentioned how God always answers prayers whether with a yes, no, or not right now, as He is planning something special for you that you may need to wait for. Included in the letter was Rosie asking if Christina would always take care of her even when she was old. I ended it with Rosie announcing that she was at our home and was waiting to meet our daughter. I placed it in an envelope and took it with me when I walked up to the school to pick up my daughter.

I met up with my daughter in the school yard and began to take a slightly different route around the other side of the school, along the side of the church, and around to the front. We sat on the church steps and I told her I had a letter I wanted her to read. I let her know it was nothing to be afraid of and that it contained some good news. She was curious and took the envelope, opened it, and began reading it. Her eyes opened wide as she began to read it quietly to herself. A huge smile appeared on her face as she continued to quickly finish reading the letter. Then she gave me back the letter, got up and started running across the church parking lot in the direction of home. I had to call her to stop and wait for me. She was visibly shaking with excitement. I was so happy to see her so overjoyed.

On the way home my daughter mentioned that the homily during the Mass at the school in the morning was about this exact topic of God hearing our prayers and answering them with yes, no, or not right now as He is planning something else. I don't think this was a coincidence. I have learned that God is in the details of our lives.

We got home the fastest we ever did while walking! I told my daughter that we should be quiet when we entered the house. She agreed and after we got settled, knowing she wanted to meet Rosie, I brought her to the second level. My daughter called Rosie's name and as if they had known each other for years, Rosie emerged immediately from behind a cabinet, walked over to my daughter, let her pat her, and then lay down beside her, purring loudly.

Somehow Rosie knew this was where she belonged, close to my daughter and my daughter had an immediate connection with Rosie. She finally had her pet, her cat, her Rosie. It was the start of something very special and has only gotten sweeter over the years.

44

Wednesday Wonders

I often attended daily Mass during the week, most often at St. Peter's Catholic Church. It is such a lovely way to start the day and the Lord always has a gift of Grace to give to you. The Wednesday Mass at St. Peter's Catholic Church in particular began to have special significance for me.

At the back of the church there was often a prayer card, pamphlet, book, small statue, Crucifix, medal, Rosary, or some other spiritual item that someone had left to share; some new and some well-loved. At first I would be hesitant to take an item, thinking it should be left for someone else. But eventually I began to see that these gifts were left for anyone to take, so why not for me now and then? They were like a special treasure I found after Mass that I could take with me to enjoy throughout the day and to have for the future. These holy reminders help to raise our hearts and minds to Heaven and the things that are above as we try our best to meet the challenges of life here on earth. They comfort us and let us know there is another realm just beyond the veil—closer than we realize.

One of the early items I was drawn to was a small stack of booklets about the story of *Our Lady of Fatima*. I was intrigued as I read the cover and flipped through the booklet. The image on the front was of Mother Mary appearing above a tree in front of three young children. I felt like I was meant to read this and so I took my graced gift home.

I began reading a little bit each night to my young daughter at bedtime. As we continued each night over several months, I began to realize how amazing this true story was. It was an action-packed drama that had really happened close to one hundred years before. The accounts of the three children, the villagers, and the investigators were captivating. My daughter and I both enjoyed learning about the true account of this miracle that happened in Fatima, Portugal in 1917.

The account of the Miracle of the Sun that was witnessed by an estimated 70,000 people was so incredible to learn about. I was inspired to do some additional research and was able to find true accounts of reports in the newspapers of the day, including the New York Times. Although it happened when my grandmother was a young adult, what occurred still has significance for our world today. I invite you to visit the website *Fatima.org* to learn more about this fascinating true story! You can find an older movie about the story online and there is a newer movie called *Fatima* that you can rent or buy.

On another Wednesday, I attended Mass and came back home to continue my day. I was working on the computer and all of a sudden I began to have this story come into my mind. It was wave after wave of images, words, and ideas so powerful that I thought I should start writing them down. The storyline came to me in a linear way as though a sequence of chapters in a book. I was so inspired by it and thought it must be another gift from God! I quickly wrote down the impressions I was receiving and the storyline as it came to me. As each scene switched I would write a few notes. Within a very short time, less than thirty minutes, I had a book outline and knew what was going to happen in each chapter. It was like a spiritual download from God!

I was amazed by it all and put it on the shelf to ponder for several months. I did eventually begin writing the book as it was given to me. I had never written a book before and it certainly had its challenges. Although I was given the storyline by God, I still had to flush out the scenes and characters. It has been a learning process and has inspired me to do other writing. I often felt interference in the writing of the book and as I look back on it I can see why the enemy would not want me to finish it. But with the grace of God I plan to finish it soon and share it as it is a beautiful story that will be especially wonderful for school children to read.

I eventually put the writing of this book to the side as I began the writing of what would become my first published book. It was based on a short story I wrote years earlier after a trip to Asia for a relative's wedding. I felt like I was meant to turn it into a book and include the parts about my reversion back to the faith and some of my struggles. Within three months the book was written and self-published. God moved fast on that project and I knew it was meant to be, and so it was! That book is titled: **To The Other Side Of The World: In The Aftermath Of 9-11**.

45

Our Lady of Fatima

I thought finding and reading the booklet about *Our Lady of Fatima* was a gift in itself but looking back now I realize that God was preparing me for another mission. On yet another graced Wednesday, I attended Mass and came home filled with joy. Within a short time after arriving home I began to have a strong thought in my mind, perhaps a locution, with the question, "What can we do for Our Lady and Our Lord?" I had recently discovered that 2017 was the hundredth anniversary of Mary Mother of God appearing to the children in Fatima in 1917 under the title of *Our Lady of Fatima*. I felt a strong call to plan something in recognition of this special event.

I was led online to discover the Rosary Rallies that take place in honour of this supernatural event. I contacted the organization in the US and they put me in touch with a Canadian organization that was helping to support Rosary Rallies in Canada. I felt like I had struck gold! I knew that I was meant to hold a Rosary Rally in honour of *Our Lady of Fatima* and thanking God for His Miracle of the Sun.

Of note, I had a friend tell me at this time that she had been given a vision of a Rosary Rally being held in our uptown park, King Square. I thought that was more than coincidence and it gave me some reassurance that I was proceeding as planned by a Higher Power.

The Rosary was given to the world from God through Mary, Mother of God, to Saint Dominic. It is contemplative prayer using beads to meditate on the life of Jesus. It brings peace and God into our midst. We can also offer special intentions for the Rosary before we begin praying. They can be announced or remain private. There were already some special intentions identified by the organization that I had connected with. I used these in addition to other intentions people offered at the local Rosary Rally.

Through word-of-mouth and some church bulletin postings we had a good turnout for the first Rosary Rally in May of 2017. I invited the children and any others who wanted to join in to begin with singing a few songs. We then prayed the Rosary, along with other prayers in the prayer booklet that I had downloaded and printed copies of. Afterwards there was fellowship, along with some snacks and drinks. It had been a beautiful sunny evening and so peaceful, I knew it was confirmation that I was meant to do this.

The Rosary Rally ran from May to October, and each month on the 13th a growing faithful group would show up. It didn't really matter the number of people in attendance but that they had made the effort to join and pray with the group.

There were so many graces, gifts, surprises, comforts, and miracles received through these Rosary Rallies that it could be its own book. Suffice to say, it has continued to be a cherished gathering each month it runs, many years later.

46

Guideposts

We had friends stop in for a visit one evening. While enjoying some snacks, refreshments, and good conversation around the kitchen table, as often happens, the topic turned to that of our shared faith.

I began to share a bit about how I had been planting some seeds by leaving prayer cards and sharing the Good News with others. My friend mentioned that she had been watching EWTN (Eternal Word Television Network—a Catholic news service) and that they had mentioned a street evangelization group. She said she thought it had St. Paul in the name. My spirit quickened within me and I made a mental note of the name, intending to look it up later.

After our guests departed and all was quiet, I decided to do a bit of research on the organization. It didn't take me long to realize that this was the perfect next step for me: to acquire formal training in Street Evangelizing and to eventually purchase some resources to hand out to people. St. Paul Street Evangelization does remarkable work providing training and materials to equip us for the mission we are called to do.

Over the next several days I explored the website and downloaded some resources. I then signed up for the Certificate in Street Evangelization training program and began working my way through the modules. I would eventually complete the course the following year.

The organization offered many faith-based resources at low cost such as medals, crucifixes, pamphlets, books, and other tools to assist in evangelization efforts. I placed my first order, which included some starter items. One of these was a box of Rosaries. The cost was incredibly low as they had volunteers who made the Rosaries. The website said that with the order I would receive a minimum of two hundred Rosaries. I thought that was an amazing deal and was looking forward to eventually passing out the Rosaries to friends, family, neighbours, and strangers.

I placed my initial order and waited patiently for it to arrive. I was not expecting what I saw the day my parcel arrived in the mail. I opened the box and saw the items I had ordered. I compared them to the packing slip as I removed each package from the large box. Below these items were the Rosaries, and I could hardly believe what I was seeing. There in front of me was what looked like a treasure chest of jewels. The Rosaries were made from colourful beads and many looked like glass gems. I was elated to see so many beautiful Rosaries. I counted them the next day and there were close to three hundred Rosaries, well above the two hundred I was expecting. I had never seen so many Rosaries in one place. It felt like I had been given a great fortune of the most wonderful kind.

With the praying of the Rosary, so many people would draw closer to God, feel Heaven's peace, receive abundant graces, and have their intentions received with love. The Rosary is a powerful spiritual weapon and I knew that each Rosary put in the hands of people to pray with would be a powerful tool of spiritual warfare that would help God in His mission to save souls. I was up for the challenge and I eventually distributed all the Rosaries and ordered more!

47

Visit Request

A few days after our friends' visit I was contacted by my oldest son. He was living in a city about an hour away. He told me his roommate was going to have a friend visit and he needed the couch that my son was sleeping on. My son had recently downsized from his own apartment and moved in with his friend to save money.

Unfortunately, it wasn't a secure situation and now he was going to be without a place to live for two weeks. Like any mother would do, I agreed to his request as I knew he was in need. I also sensed there were other struggles he was having and I thought a visit with me would give him some stability while waiting.

Due to scheduling conflicts and my husband's need of our car for business, I was looking for alternatives to get my son to our home for the visit. I had a good friend who offered to drive me to pick up my son. That was such a generous offer and I was so thankful. As the days passed, she decided that to make more space available in the car, she would let me borrow her car to drive on my own. I was so grateful for her generosity and trust. Deep down I was sensing something else was going on and that my son was coming home to be protected for a while. My friend and I prayed together for safety and protection and off I went with my daughter to pick up my son.

When we arrived, we began moving some of his items to the car. Without speaking, I somehow knew that we were going to be taking most if not all of his belongings. He had gone to university in this city and had previously lived in a furnished apartment so he hadn't accumulated a lot of big items like furniture. But even without furniture, he still managed to acquire many items for daily living, work, hobbies, and a few favourites along the way. We began to place box after box into the car which was a seven-seater with lots of space. In came clothes, jackets, shoes, computer equipment, and music gear, and within a short time the car was packed with just enough space for the three of us.

We drove home and unpacked the car as I needed to return it to my friend. I thanked her for the gift of her car and let her know I had refilled the tank with gas, which was all she had requested. No borrowing fee—just the simplest request to refill the tank. I was so thankful for her friendship!

The following week after my son had settled in for his visit, he mentioned that he would really like to have his bike so that he could get around in the city. He didn't have a driver's license yet and he had enjoyed the biking in the city he had been living in. I didn't know how or when I would ever be able to get us back there and thought he might have to save up for a new bike. We just didn't have room for it the first trip nor did I have a bike rack.

I happened to mention this bike issue in passing to my friend, and she quickly offered the car for me to borrow again. I couldn't believe it! Here she was once more, selflessly meeting the need of my son, someone she did not know. I gratefully accepted her offer and let my son know. He was deeply appreciative of her generosity too.

Within a few days my son, daughter and I travelled to retrieve his bike. We played with another neighbour's dog outside for a while, took a short walk on a trail, and then loaded up the bike. There was a feeling of emptiness and transience in this place. It didn't have roots and I questioned if it had wings. It felt lifeless and I was relieved to be departing with my son and his bike. Deep down I didn't think he would ever return and that gave me a profound sense of peace. I thought God had other plans for my son and I was the link at that moment. One day at a time is all I could do.

It was easier to unpack this time with only a bike to lock up outside. I returned my friend's car to her with another full tank of gas and a big thank you. I will always remember her kindness and generosity in my eldest son's time of need. She has been a good friend to me and I am so thankful to have her in my life. We need more people like this in the world: those who go beyond the basic expectations in life, who go outside their comfort zone and meet what are oftentimes unexpected and difficult needs.

48

Saint Thérèse of Lisieux Novena

My son had been struggling before he requested to stay with us for the two weeks. He had become burnt out from his tech support job, had reduced his hours to part-time, and then his job was cut. He had gone on employment insurance but that had run out. It doesn't take long to become vulnerable in our lives. It was a reminder of how easily anyone can quickly become homeless.

When experiencing this vulnerability oftentimes we are more open to ways we can get a hand up to improve our situation. It seemed to me that my son was relieved to be staying with us and it was going to give him a reprieve from dealing with the stress of unemployment. He was interested in starting his own business and so I encouraged him to go in that direction.

Having a deep faith now, I could see that my son needed so much more than a job. He needed to come to know Jesus. I felt that my son had come to stay with me for a while so that I could share the Good News with him. When my son was growing up I was away from the church and so he did not receive instruction in the faith except for the occasional time his grandparents would take him to church. I had deep regrets about not raising him to truly be close to God. Sometimes I would talk about how God is in Heaven and someday we will go to live there forever if we are good on earth. But mentioning God now and then is far from what we are called to do in the raising of our children. Children need to know how close God is to them, how much He loves and cares for them, what His Commandments and teachings are, and how they can rely on Him for help in their lives through faith and prayer and the Bible. They also need to know and partake of the Sacraments of the Church which will strengthen them and provide grace for the journey.

> Train up a child in the way he should go: and when he is old, he will not depart from it. (Proverbs 22:6)

Now that my son was grown up and still without that solid base I was in a sense trying to get him to climb a mountain. But I decided to be his Sherpa guide and begin at base camp. Throughout my home on walls, tables, and shelves were many holy reminders including statues, framed prints, prayer cards, medals, and Rosaries—that was a good start for my son. I had nothing to lose in doing what I could to help win my son's soul over to become one of God's children and so I wasted no time. I gently gave my son a Crucifix which he accepted. Next came a Miraculous Medal. Then a Rosary, some prayer cards, another medal. He was collecting some blessed items that were spiritually powerful and he was receptive to them.

Amazingly he let me Baptize him right in our kitchen. I knew the chances of getting my son into a church at this point were slim and knowing we were living in the End Times and realizing anything can happen in our lives, I felt an urgency to provide an "Emergency Baptism." I had Holy Water and the required prayers to do this, and given that I am his mother, now with a strong faith, I was the one closest to him to provide this essential spiritual act of love. It was truly a Miracle that this happened and I am thankful for God's leading.

We had good discussions about the faith and he was definitely asking a lot of questions. I did my best to answer the questions to the best of my knowledge. Sometimes I would find additional information and email it to him. Sometimes he asked such complex questions that they were difficult for me to answer and I would make a list of them intending to ask a priest or to do some deeper research on his behalf.

Bottom line: He wanted verifiable proof of the existence of God. It sounded a bit like a science experiment yet at the same time seemed to be a reasonable request. Science has been able to prove the existence of God in many ways, including through independent forensic lab testing of Eucharistic Miracles. No one wants to be fooled into believing something that is not real. I got that. Having a deep faith myself, I was aware that no one should be prevented from discovering and knowing the truth. Everyone has a deep desire and a right to know the truth about where they came from, why they are here, and where they may go when their life is finished here.

As I was searching through some of my prayer cards, I came across the Saint Thérèse of Lisieux Novena. It had a beautiful image on the front of St. Thérèse holding a Crucifix and some pink roses. On the back was a Novena—a nine-day prayer. The Novena is based on the nine days that Jesus' disciples along with Holy Mother Mary waited in the Upper Room for the Holy Spirit to arrive on the day of Pentecost—signalling the formal beginning of the Church.

We often pray and ask our Holy Helpers in Heaven to intercede for us. Because God has created us to be one big family, He delights in His Saints being a part of helping with earthly requests. There are hundreds of Novenas in honour of various saints for different purposes. This one is a well-known Novena with St. Thérèse as our intercessor.

Novena to Saint Thérèse of Lisieux

O Little Thérèse of the Child Jesus, please pick for me a rose from the heavenly gardens and send it to me as a message of love.

O Little Flower of Jesus, ask God to grant the favours I now place with confidence in your hands...

(Mention in silence here)

St. Thérèse, help me to always believe as you did in God's great love for me, so that I might imitate your 'Little Way' each day.

Amen

I felt a deep knowing that I was meant to use this Novena in some way for my oldest son. I had a talk with my daughter and asked her if she would be willing to pray this Novena with her brother. I told her that I thought he would be more receptive to praying it if it was something he and his sister were doing, without Mom being a part of it. She agreed and so I asked my son if he was willing to pray this Novena with his sister. I explained that it was for nine days and that he could make a prayer request. He agreed to pray it and he was at peace about it, even a little bit hopeful. Of course, his prayer request was to obtain verifiable proof of the existence of God. I thought, what does he have to lose? I am certain St. Thérèse will be able to help us.

They both prayed the prayer that first evening, and each evening afterwards. There was one evening when I asked my daughter later in the evening if she and her brother had prayed the Novena. She looked concerned as she answered, "No." She quickly went to the basement door and invited my son upstairs to the kitchen to pray, which he readily agreed to. All was going well. I even made a small checklist to ensure they prayed for the complete nine days. I also prayed a few prayers during this time hoping to boost their prayers with my faith. I was hoping that God would reveal something special to my son that would open up his heart and mind to the existence of a Higher Power—his Creator and Saviour, Jesus!

49

Morning Mass

The day after the Novena to St. Thérèse was completed was a Wednesday…August 16, 2017, to be exact. I was running the Sunbeams program and on this day we were starting with the 9:00 am Mass at St. Peter's Catholic Church. In addition to my daughter, there would be three other children joining us. I recall it was a beautiful, warm and sunny day as we waited outside the church for all the children to arrive. When all had gathered we went inside the church to wait for the Mass to begin. There weren't very many people in the church as it was a weekday Mass. Most were middle-aged or older adults. The Mass began and we entered into the mystery of Love itself.

50

Two Strangers

When Mass was finished, the children and I walked towards the door. I recall the church's main doors were opened wide—a beacon of welcome for those walking by and a scene of beauty for those leaving the church after Mass. The brightness of the sunlight and blue sky above the tall trees with their green fullness welcomed us out of the dimly lit church into the new day.

As we exited the church and stepped down to the top landing, I noticed two people walking across the parking lot pavement at the bottom of the stairs. It was perfect timing—they were just stepping across my view as I was looking down. Always on the lookout for people I could share some Good News with, I quickly said, "Good morning." I recall the older of the two looked up at me and replied with an appreciative smile. Having just received Jesus in the Eucharist at Mass, I was filled with His Spirit and Love and wanted to share it with others.

The children and I walked down the stairs towards the two strangers. I was well aware that this could be another opportunity to share a Kingdom Message. Upon first glance I noted they were both men and unfamiliar to me. I continued to observe them as I made my way down the stairs with the children.

The older man looked to be in his mid to late forties. He was wearing jeans, a buttoned jean jacket, and brown leather sandals. He had layered shoulder length brown hair with a few gray streaks through it and a shadow beard and moustache. His eyes were brown and his skin was fair. He was tall, about six feet, and with a slim, fit build. He had a knapsack on his back that was packed and I noticed a tin cup sticking out of the top. The tin cup was so shiny; it looked brand new. He also had a guitar in a case on his back. He struck me as though he was a travelling musician, a bit of a wanderer who enjoyed exploring new places. I sensed he was a kind person, down to earth, and quiet.

The second man looked to be in his early twenties. He was wearing jeans too and had on a white t-shirt with a sports team emblem on it. He was wearing white sneakers and he too had a guitar case slung over his back. His hair was shoulder length, brown, and curly and his eyes were brown. He had a roundish face, giving him a youthful appearance. He was quiet and remained in the background as I continued the conversation with the older man.

I commented on the beautiful sunny day we were enjoying. I then told them my name. The older of the two introduced himself as Robert and the other as Elijah. When I heard the Biblical name, it struck me deeply. I thought it fitting that I was meeting someone with this unique Biblical name in front of the church.

51

Show Hospitality

I thought there was more going on behind the scenes that I was meant to explore. The only way to find out was to keep talking and asking questions to see where it would lead. Robert shared that he had been in Nova Scotia—that he had some land there. I asked Elijah if they were friends. He replied that they had met the day before and that they were spending some time together. They were enjoying playing music together on their guitars. For having met each other just the day before, from what I could observe they had become fast friends.

They did mention that they wanted to get some coffee. It was morning, and they hadn't had any breakfast yet. I am not sure if they had been walking all night or had found a place to lay their head. I was trying to help where I could but didn't want to pry. Since they were not from my city, they were unfamiliar with where the local coffee shops were. I mentioned a couple of places they could get coffee nearby. They didn't seem in a hurry to leave, as though they were lingering for some other reason yet to be revealed.

I continued to chat with them, sharing that I was operating a summer childcare program out of the church hall. I let them know that it was an enrichment program that included art. I then segued this to the two guitars that were in front of me. I love music, as do most people, especially children. I was thinking why miss an opportunity to hear live music. I decided to ask Robert and Elijah if they would consider playing a song for the children. Without any hesitation they both agreed. I was delighted they were willing to share their music with us.

I then invited them to meet the children in my program. Always aware of the children's safety especially around strangers, I was optimistically cautious. I also wanted to model good manners for the children in being welcoming to others while in this safe environment. This was a wonderful opportunity to provide an example to the children of being friendly to those we meet and not being fearful of strangers just because we don't know them. The age-old advice *don't talk to strangers* can certainly hold up well in certain situations but in a safe place with their leader, it isn't necessary nor fitting.

I was thinking about the Bible verse about showing hospitality to strangers. Not only is it a kind thing to do, but God also wants us to do it, and we might receive a blessing in return whether in this life or the next. It is another form of love for our brothers and sisters and it is good for us to look beyond our concerns to the needs of others. We also might learn something interesting about the stranger and perhaps be given insights and wisdom to help us on our own journey. There is always the possibility of a stranger becoming a friend, after all the friends we have now were once strangers.

There was also the possibility that we could be *entertaining angels*! All the more reason to always welcome the stranger. I wondered how many times I *had* entertained angels in the past. There have been a few times in my adult life where I have encountered people for a fleeting moment that made me wonder if they were angels in disguise.

Do not neglect to show hospitality to strangers, for by doing that some have entertained angels without knowing it. (Hebrews 13:2)

52

Fatherly

I began to introduce Robert and Elijah to the children. Once again Elijah hung in the background and I didn't want to force an uncomfortable introduction so I focused on Robert who had moved closer.

The first child that I introduced was the oldest, about twelve at the time. While watching closely, I noticed that Robert shook her hand and then offered to give her a hug. She willingly gave him a friendly hug, but I could sense a bit of awkwardness on her part. I then overheard Robert say to her, "Hug me like I am your father." I then observed that she gave him a warmer hug, not so awkward this time. She was a mature and assertive girl and if she did not want to hug him, she would not have. I was ready to step in to say that I would rather he not hug the children but I did not think there was any particular risk at the moment. He then offered a few encouraging words to her and moved on to the next child.

I knew from my interactions with the next child that she was a bit distant from God and her faith. When Robert shook her hand I noted he did not move to hug her. He looked kindly on her and spoke to her about letting more light into her life. It was a gentle instruction but I was amazed at how true his words were.

He continued down the line with the other children, shaking their hands and offering an encouraging word. I pondered who this person was who would take time to speak with loving directness to each child with words of wisdom.

Of special note, the oldest girl who I introduced Robert to first had moved to Canada with her mother and siblings the year before. Her mother was accepted into an advanced program at a local learning centre. Their father was still in their home country, hoping to eventually move to Canada with his family when the conditions were right. That very morning this girl had been missing her father in a very deep way. She shared this with me later in the day and expressed the comfort she felt in hearing Robert's words.

53

On The Right Track

When Robert was finished speaking his special words to the children he moved towards me and stood in front of me on the main steps of the church. All of a sudden, he began speaking these words to me:

"Keep doing what you're doing. You're on the right track."

I didn't really know what to say, and so I said, "Thank you." I looked at him, wondering if he was sent from Heaven to deliver this message to me. It was a confirmation that I needed to hear as I had been wondering if I *was* on the right track—if my meandering life was leading in the right direction. I received the message as a gift and felt reassurance and peace.

54

Singing Over Me

Next both Robert and Elijah moved to the first landing of the stairs with their guitars. I was so grateful that they were willing to play a song for us without me having to remind them or ask again. I didn't want them to feel obligated to. Each with their own guitars, they probably enjoyed playing for others.

I called the children to come closer as Robert and Elijah were going to play a song for us. The children gathered in with curiosity and eagerness to hear a song on the guitar. What happened next was very unexpected.

Robert began to play the guitar *and* to sing along. I hadn't thought that he might also have a singing ability but often they go together. The song he sang and played was so beautiful. I had never heard it before and perhaps it was his original. It had many verses and was like a story—with thoughtful lyrics that touched my heart. I also recall there was a reference to God in it which was comforting.

It was as though the song was a gift coming to us from Heaven through Robert. I knew this was something so out of the ordinary and so I continued to be attentive to every note of this stirring song and its singer.

> The Lord your God is with you, the Mighty Warrior who saves. He will take great delight in you; in his love he will no longer rebuke you but will rejoice over you with singing.
> (Zephaniah 3:17)

55

Maintenance Check

Partway through the song I saw another one of the church doors open at the top of the left stairs. There were three sets of stairs at the front of the church and our group was on the main steps leading to the centre doors. The church caretaker stuck his head out and looked in our direction. He probably heard the music playing from the main doors that were wide open. I lifted my hands towards our guests and then raised them toward the sky to indicate that this was something rare and beautiful—a gift from Heaven. I am not sure if he recognized my signal, but I noted he scanned the outdoors and then returned inside the church.

56

Double Gift

After Robert finished singing we all clapped and said thank you. It was such a beautiful song to listen to and if that had been the only song we heard that day it would have been enough. But as soon as he finished I noticed Elijah was getting his guitar out of the case. I looked at him and asked if he was going to play a song for us too. He replied, "Yes," then began to strum his guitar and sing for us.

Once again it was a deeply moving song with a beautiful melody and lyrics. His voice was so soothing to listen to. There were several verses to the song and the lyrics of one of the verses touched me deeply and personally. I was overflowing with peace, love, and gratitude. The children clapped afterwards and we thanked our guests for their musical gifts to us. We were all doubly blessed with these two amazing songs and their gift givers.

57

True Presence

Robert and Elijah didn't seem in a hurry to leave us just yet and so I asked if they would like to see the inside of the church to which they readily agreed. Up the remaining steps we went, along with the children. We all entered through the open bright red double doors to the peaceful interior of the church.

Mindful that Jesus is truly present in the Tabernacles of all Catholic churches, including this one, I wanted our guests to be informed of this important truth. I also wanted to honour my Lord and not to ignore His presence. Tabernacles are usually ornamental gold boxes that are either at the centre of the altar or to the side in a prominent place of honour.

As Catholics, we believe that through the special prayers of a priest, he is able to take unleavened bread and, invoking the power of the Holy Spirit through the words of Consecration, turn the bread into the Body, Blood, Soul, and Divinity of Jesus Christ. Jesus instituted this himself at the Last Supper on Holy Thursday over two thousand years ago, on the night before He was crucified on the cross. Jesus gave his apostles (the first priests) this power and it has been continually transmitted through two thousand years during the Bishop's laying on of hands at every priestly ordination.

Any extra consecrated hosts not used for Communion at the Holy Sacrifice of the Mass are stored in the Tabernacle for another Mass, special services, or for Adoration. There is always at least one Communion host in the Tabernacle so that the True Presence is always in the church and visitors can come before the Tabernacle to pray, knowing Jesus is with them.

As simply as I could, I explained that Jesus was present in the Tabernacle under the appearance of bread but it was truly His Body, Blood, Soul, and Divinity in the Consecrated Host. Robert looked in the direction of the Tabernacle and then he turned towards the open double-doors, scanning the blue sky, and then said quietly but with authority, "God is everywhere." I asked him to repeat what he said as I was surprised at his response and wanted to make sure I had heard him correctly. He repeated it and then I told him, "Yes, I agree, God *is* everywhere."

It seemed for a moment as though I was trying to put God in a box, figuratively and maybe spiritually. God cannot be contained; He is all powerful, all knowing, and omnipresent. Coming before the True Presence of Christ in a Tabernacle is one way we can encounter Him. I really wasn't trying to diminish God by sharing this with Robert, but from that day on, I was reminded that God *is* everywhere and we can find Him inside *and* outside of a church in a multitude of ways.

> "Am I only a God nearby," declares the Lord, "and not a God far away? Who can hide in secret places so that I cannot see them?" declares the Lord. "Do not I fill heaven and earth?" declares the Lord. (Jeremiah 23:23-24)

58

Higher Words

I observed the children were just off to the side huddled together and I was thinking we would be leaving the church shortly. Then all of a sudden I became aware of Robert moving purposely in front of me. I was facing the front of the church at this point just at the beginning of the church pews. He looked intently at me and then began to speak directly to me.

He raised both of his arms and began to move them in a circular motion as he shared these words:

"In Heaven, an emerald rainbow surrounds the throne. There is a fiery throne of God and there, wheels go round and round and fiery flames of love come off the throne and go out to the world. These flames of love go down to the earth and into families. Love in a family is important. This love goes between a husband and wife and through them to the children. If there is not enough love, there can be depression and anger."

As he was saying this I recall hearing something about wheels of fire in Heaven in a recent Bible reading at Mass. But to hear it explained this way made it seem more profound and with a deeper meaning. It was as though Robert was communicating a message to me from Heaven. It struck a chord with me as I have not always felt "enough love" in my family, whether my family of origin or the family I have tried my best to form as an adult. I also know I have fallen short of always demonstrating love to others. This is an almost universal experience for most people.

I wasn't sure what to say but it was as though Robert somehow knew what I have experienced in my life and what I was currently going through and so I replied with a bit of resignation:

"I am trying my best."

He just looked at me with his peaceful and wise countenance and said nothing more. His words to me were profound and left me in wonder. This is the related Bible passage:

> "As I looked, "thrones were set in place, and the Ancient of Days took his seat. His clothing was as white as snow; the hair of his head was white like wool. His throne was flaming with fire, and its wheels were all ablaze. A river of fire was flowing, coming out from before him. Thousands upon thousands attended him; ten thousand times ten thousand stood before him. The court was seated, and the books were opened. (Daniel 7:9-10)

This is the related Bible passage about the emerald rainbow around the throne in Heaven:

> At once I was in the spirit, and there in heaven stood a throne, with one seated on the throne! And the one seated there looks like jasper and carnelian, and around the throne is a rainbow that looks like an emerald. (Revelation 4:2-3)

Of note, I decided to do a bit of research on jasper and carnelian referenced in the above Bible passage. I discovered that jasper is a mineral, most commonly the colour red. Carnelian is another mineral that is most often red or orange. These colours reminded me of the fiery flames of love that come off the throne of God in Heaven.

59

Coffee Invite

I announced to the children that we were going out of the church. We all went to the bottom of the church stairs and I was thinking we were going to get ready to say goodbye to Robert and Elijah.

Robert mentioned the coffee again and that they were going to get some nearby. Then instantly I thought why not invite them to my home for coffee. I thought it would be more welcoming than for them to go to a coffee shop with strangers. My adult son was still visiting us and I thought if there were any problems he could help me. But I didn't think there would be any concerns. In the back of my mind I was hoping that Robert might have some additional words to share with my oldest son. I was beginning to think that I was *entertaining angels*.

I then officially invited Robert and Elijah for coffee at my house. I made a reference to my son who could help me make the coffee. I wanted them to know there was an adult male currently in my house so they knew what and whom to expect. I told them we were within walking distance of about 10-15 minutes, depending on how fast the children walked. Their response was one of complete agreement with no obvious feeling of obligation or uncomfortableness. It was as though Robert and Elijah were *meant* to visit my home.

60

Skip in His Step

I let the children know that Robert and Elijah were coming to my house for coffee with us and that they would be staying for a short visit. The children acknowledged our plans and seemed curious and happy about our kind acquaintances coming back with us for a little while.

I had the children line up with the youngest in front and my daughter in the back. My daughter was my little helper and assisted with many aspects of the Sunbeams program, including making sure the children were staying in line and being well-behaved. I always led the line for direction, and safety—especially for crossing roads. I began to walk and the children followed.

Our guests were walking with us in no particular order, but once we crossed a couple of roads at the intersection and were walking down the sidewalk I noticed that Elijah was walking beside me at the front of the line and Robert was walking at the end of the line, behind my daughter. I was chatting with Elijah as we walked along, telling him a bit about the neighbourhood, and making chitchat about general topics.

I heard Robert chatting a bit with the children as we went along. I didn't hear everything but the children did mention to me later that he had told them that he had some land in Nova Scotia that he had recently bought and that some day we could visit him.

As we all walked along, I looked back several times making sure the children were following and that everything was going smoothly. Upon one of these glances back I observed an obvious joy on Robert's face. He seemed so happy walking with us and he had a skip in his step. He was looking at the children walking before him as though they were his and he was content to be in their company. It was pure innocent love and with the sun shining on him and the children it was so beautiful to observe.

Special moments don't cost anything. We often think we need a trip, a ticket, a big plan to enjoy our days but often it truly is in the quiet and simple moments of life when true joy can be experienced and special memories made. This child-like walk and talk is forever etched in my memory as one of true joy—for Robert, for me and I hope for the children, and Elijah.

> ...He said to them, "Let the little children come to me, and do not hinder them, for the kingdom of God belongs to such as these. Truly I tell you, anyone who will not receive the kingdom of God like a little child will never enter it." (Mark 10:14-15)

61

Stop to Smell the Roses

As we were nearing the bend in the road I heard Robert point out the beautiful pink rose bush to the children. It was a large bush on the front of a neighbour's lawn close to the edge of the sidewalk, filled with exquisite blooms and stunning to behold. Robert was observing this too and clearly didn't want to walk by without paying some attention to the beautiful scene.

Robert touched one of the flowers and breathed in the scent. He then invited the children to smell the roses too and they all gathered around the rose bush to enjoy its beauty and scent. There were also a few buzzing bees to add to the experience—and thankfully, no bee stings. Seeing the colour and beauty of the blooms, touching their soft petals, and smelling their subtle scent helped the children to connect with and appreciate nature.

There are so many ways to engage children in their environment, to teach them, to help them to slow down and enjoy nature. This doesn't cost anything but a little time and effort and can fill them with appreciation and gratitude for the simple wonders around them.

Robert clearly knew this and he helped the children to truly savour this beautiful moment in time together.

62

Litter Lesson

We continued on our way to the end of the next road and turned onto a main street. All of sudden I became aware that Robert was stooping down to pick up garbage off the sidewalk. There was some miscellaneous garbage that had made its way to the sidewalk, possibly on a windy day whether due to someone purposely littering, or someone putting their garbage out too early and a creature tearing a hole in the bag.

The neighbourhood I lived in was not my first choice but chosen through circumstances beyond our control. The redeeming part of living here was that it was within walking distance of the church we attended for years and the school our daughter attended throughout her primary education. It was also within walking distance to shops and services, a grocery store, parks, playgrounds, walking trails, the river, and the ocean. It had a lot of potential and slowly developers and investors were buying up property and making positive changes in the neighbourhood.

It was a low-income area of our city and there were problems in the area, including unemployment, addictions, mental health, criminal activity, and other issues. I had noted a garbage issue when we had moved to the area a few years before. Trying to do my part, I had gone out with my daughter to pick up garbage around where we lived. It inspired a few neighbours to help and it didn't take long until our street started to look better. But unless everyone is doing their part and being vigilant about when and where to put garbage out, problems with litter persist. Here we were with our very own guest doing his part to pick up some of the litter.

I apologized to Robert for the litter and then I thought once again it could be a learning and serving opportunity for the children. So I announced to the children that we were going to help Robert pick up some litter. Always having extra plastic bags with me to reuse, I quickly pulled out one for each child. I instructed them to use it like a glove and to only pick up something like paper or packaging—nothing sharp or unfamiliar. So we all picked up a piece and then I combined it all into my bag.

It seems like enough to take care of our own garbage, but I admire those who help clean up someone else's neighbourhood. It is a humble and helpful service in areas where there may not be much appreciation for the importance of keeping a neighbourhood litter-free. All our neighbourhoods are connected into one city and we must all do our part to keep these spaces clean.

63

Hogweed

Since I could tell that Robert was a nature lover and environmentalist, I thought he might have some insight into an overgrowth of plants that I had noted over the past couple of years in the vacant valley behind which we were now standing.

I told him what I had learned about the overgrowth of plants there and that they were related to the giant hogweed. I had heard many warnings about the hogweed family of plants: if the sap gets on the skin and is exposed to sunlight, painful blisters can develop that can last from weeks to months. Even more serious: if the sap gets in one's eyes it can cause blindness. Whenever I walked by these plants, I always made sure we stayed clear of it as there was some close to the sidewalk. Once again on this day, I strongly warned the children not to go near any of the plants along the sidewalk—reiterating the reasons why.

Robert quietly listened to what I shared about these dangerous plants and then he said, "It is because of the area." I noted he was scanning the neighbourhood while he said this and I could tell his face had much less peacefulness to it than earlier at the rose bush. I sensed there was something more to what he was saying and I asked questions to clarify. I asked if it was because of the spiritual state of the area. He affirmed this with a quiet but firm, "Yes."

I then immediately made the connection that the overgrowth of this toxic plant was in relation to the behaviours, choices, and issues of many living in the area and that somehow it was affecting the local nature. It was as though nature was manifesting the spiritual state of the area. I wanted to have clarification about my theory and so I asked bluntly, "Do you mean sin?" Robert answered with a resigned, "Yes."

Having lived in the area already for a few years, I could see sin *was* prevalent in many ways. There was a serious drug issue in the area, lots of drinking and loud parties, loud music, foul language, theft, vandalism, questionable living arrangements, hostility, and certainly not loving one's neighbour very well. My family had been affected by much of this negativity and so I knew firsthand there was a lot of improvement needed, much of it connected to the spiritual state of souls living here.

I have since observed this overgrowth of plants in other areas of the city and in other cities and out of province, and often in "nice neighbourhoods." Perhaps it is in a state of overgrowth all over the world where it can grow, signalling the spiritual state of many areas. Maybe there are other plants in other parts of the world that are unnaturally overgrowing with the same message. Nature has a connection to the divine and has been and continues to be affected by the fall of Adam and Eve in the Garden, and humanity's continuous and increasing sinning. If we want to help to make creation beautiful again, let us consider sinning less or not at all, repenting if we do sin, trying to do better in all areas of our lives, and loving God, our families, and our neighbours more, a lot more.

I am not here to make judgements on people. I will let God do His job as He is the final judge. I can make pronouncements on what I have observed and make a basic comparison with how God really wants us to live our lives. If we all take a hard look at our lives, we will all conclude that we have all sinned (done wrong), are in sin or will sin in the future—whether it is something that is observable by others or so-called hidden sin that we think we are concealing or justifying but we must remember that God sees all. Until we breathe our final breath, we still have time to amend our lives, to repent to God and others (apologize, ask forgiveness, make amends, and turn away from sin) for our wrongdoing and to get on the right path that will lead to good here on the earth and in the afterlife. This I do know for sure: There *is* a Heaven and you don't want to miss it!

> For the creation waits with eager longing for the revealing of the children of God; for the creation was subjected to futility, not of its own will but by the will of the one who subjected it, in hope that the **creation itself will be set free from its bondage to decay** and will obtain the freedom of the glory of the children of God. We know that the whole creation has been groaning in labour pains until now; and not only the creation, but we ourselves, who have the first fruits of the Spirit, groan inwardly while we wait for adoption, the redemption of our bodies. (Romans 8:19-23)

64

Like a Friend

We continued on the final stretch to my home. Once we arrived we remained outside for a few minutes enjoying the sun. I noticed that Robert was now talking directly to me as though he was a good friend. He began sharing again that he had land in Nova Scotia that he had just bought and that we could visit him there in the future. I thought it a bit strange that he was referring to land in the next province over and making plans for the future while hardly even knowing me.

Then I thought he is probably one of those friendly people who once they meet you are your friend for life. Well, here I was inviting two strangers to my home for coffee, so perhaps he was wanting to reciprocate. I tried my best to stay open to the possibilities as this day was unfolding. Of note, my parents were born in Nova Scotia and I have several relatives there, and I attended university there, and have visited often. We enjoyed traveling and visiting relatives as I was growing up and as an adult. I have always felt like a Cape Bretoner at heart.

65

Coffee Time

We all went into the house. I told the children to wash their hands then eat their snacks. I suggested they could take out a game on the second level to play for a while. We had lots of board games for the children to choose from and they were always enthusiastic about playing a game together. I told them I was going to make coffee for our guests who would be visiting for a little while.

As we were moving from the foyer to the kitchen, I noted Robert looked at the Crucifix on the wall as he went by. I wondered what he thought about it and all the other reminders of my faith. It was clear that he was a believer in God, I just wasn't sure if he was a supporter of the Catholic faith or another Christian denomination. He was a free spirit and speaking as he did about God being everywhere, perhaps he preferred a less structured way of living and believing.

I realized that it was coffee time and I knew I was not a coffee shop barista. I had long ago worked in restaurants in Toronto while attending college but never got past the drip coffee maker with its prepackaged ground coffee. My husband knew how to make a great cup of coffee and had made thousands over the years, many shared with me. In fact, he was really a coffee connoisseur. He often made coffee using his French press. He would put coffee grounds in a glass jar, fill with boiling water, push the metal strainer partway down, wait for the required time, strain the coffee grounds, pour the coffee, add any extras like flavoured milk and then enjoy it! I occasionally made coffee using the French press at home, but I always double-checked with my husband on the process.

I was definitely a novice at making this type of coffee and a bit nervous about messing it up and serving a terrible cup of coffee to my guests. I was hoping my son could help me make a good cup of coffee for Robert and Elijah as he sometimes made coffee with the French press too. I also wanted to invite my son up to meet our guests with hopes that there might be a special word from Robert to share with him.

I called down to my son inviting him to come up to meet our guests. Now, I know it was a long shot but you just never know when your young adult son might agree to your request. He was still sleeping and declined immediately. I then asked if he could come up to at least help me use the coffee press as I was not that familiar with it. My son declined again and told me the instructions were on the side of the glass coffee press. I lifted up the coffee press to see the instructions printed in white on the side. I was going to have to read these instructions and follow them exactly to make the perfect coffee. I was not sure if I wanted to serve my guests the in-training cup of coffee.

I looked over and saw Robert leaning against the kitchen counter with his arms crossed, looking like he was deep in thought. Elijah was quietly in the background as he always seemed to be. I thought I would attempt to make the coffee according to the printed instructions and so I put some water in the kettle to boil.

As I was beginning to get cups out, I looked over and noticed Robert was no longer there. I asked Elijah where he went and he replied that he had gone outside. I thought that was a bit odd but thought he was just enjoying the sunny day while I made coffee.

As I was chatting a bit with Elijah, I asked him where he was from and he told me Cape Breton. I replied, "Really? My parents are from Cape Breton." Thinking of a good breakfast for my new friends, I asked if he liked porridge and he said, "Yes." I asked if he and Robert would like a bowl of oatmeal for breakfast and he replied, "Yes."

I went to the foyer and looked out the window to check for Robert but I couldn't see him in the front of my home. Elijah went out and came back in a short time later to let me know that Robert was talking to the workers next door who were doing some renovations to the building. I thought that since Robert was so down-to-earth and friendly that he was just getting to know some more people.

I was mixing the oatmeal into the boiling water in the pot and got the brown sugar out of the cupboard. All of a sudden I felt a shift in the atmosphere. Elijah was looking towards the foyer with expectancy. He went out the door for a minute and then returned to tell me that they had to go. There was an urgency in his voice and I could somehow tell that their time at our house was coming to a quick close. I asked if he had time to eat the porridge and as I could tell they would be leaving soon, I suggested that I could put the porridge in a container to go. Elijah agreed and so I prepared the porridge with milk and brown sugar in a bowl with a plastic spoon for him to take. He then moved towards the door and began to eat the porridge quickly. I then said I would get a bowl ready for Robert. But Elijah said, "No, that's alright, I can share my porridge with Robert." I thought they must be in a real hurry, so I didn't bother with a second bowl.

I then saw Robert through the glass of the front door. He was hurrying up the steps to the unlocked door. I noted he was wearing a lime green t-shirt which must have been under his jean jacket that he removed as it was so hot out now. He opened the door and came in, announcing,

"We have to leave." I replied, "Alright, it was nice to have met you and Elijah." We hugged each other and then I hugged Elijah.

Robert then said to me, "Bring down the children. I want to say good-bye to them." I thought that was a kind gesture and that he seemed like such a gentleman to offer a formal farewell before departing. I called up to the children and asked them to come down as our guests were now leaving and we were going to say good-bye to them.

Robert went outside first to wait for me to bring the children out. Knowing I had but a short time, I asked Elijah if he went to church. He told me he used to but hadn't for a while. I gave him one of my prayer cards telling him Jesus was real and He was soon returning. Elijah received it and said thank you and went outside to wait with Robert.

The children all came down, put their shoes on, and we all went outside to say our good-byes. Robert asked for the children to line up at the bottom of the stairs on the grass. He said it as though he was a teacher instructing the children with authority and kindness. The children willingly lined up and I was nearby keeping watch over everyone.

Robert then spoke to each child for a few moments. He began with a little girl asking her if she liked to write stories, to which she agreed. He encouraged her to keep writing and then he pulled a pen out of his pocket and gave it to her.

Next was the girl who I thought could draw closer to Jesus in her life. Robert spoke with her and suggested she keep searching for more light in her life. He told her that if she found herself in darkness that this would help. He then pulled out a small flashlight and handed it to her. She thanked him and moved to the side with the first girl.

The next girl Robert spoke to was a very responsible child. Robert said that she seemed to be the type of person that liked to keep her feet steady on the ground and to know where she was going, to which she agreed. He then told her that if she were not sure of what direction to take, that this could help, and he pulled a compass out of his pocket and gave it to her. I was amazed at his accuracy of words as they would not apply as closely to the other children as they did to her.

The final girl was my daughter. Robert asked if she played any musical instruments. She hesitated and I helped her by saying she could play the violin a bit, the ukulele, the piano, but most importantly she loved to sing and that her voice was her favourite instrument. Robert then told her to keep singing and enjoying music. He then pulled out a harmonica from his pocket and handed it to her. I was amazed at what had just occurred. A musical instrument was so fitting for her talent as she truly had a golden voice and had participated in many musical endeavours. She had taken voice lessons for many years, sang in her school choir, my Sunbeams choir, community fundraisers, and had also entered the provincial music festival several times. Her father and I had grown up with music ourselves and our home was always filled with a variety of music.

66

Back to Ontario

Robert then mentioned that he had to get back to his wife in Ontario. I had noticed a golden band on his ring finger earlier and thought he was married. He mentioned the land in Nova Scotia again and that we could visit him there sometime. He was inviting us all collectively yet keeping the *how* and *when* a bit of a mystery. I was wondering how that might happen but stayed open to the possibility. I replied, "Yes, we might be able to do that in the future." I have learned over my lifetime not to shut something down too quickly. Allowing some time to think about an offer, invitation, or other occurrence that is out of the ordinary may be a blessing in disguise.

Robert then looked at me intensely and said, "I will see you next summer or later this year." Again, trying my best to be hospitable, I responded, "Yes that would be nice." I was thinking that he was very friendly and seemed sincere. He was planning to now include us as an additional stop on his way to or from Nova Scotia.

I recall making a mental note of what he said so that I would know the time parameters and whether he would try to contact me or come to my house while passing through. We didn't exchange contact information but he now knew where I lived and could always knock on my door. I never felt like pulling out my cell phone to take a photo as these two people were really strangers and I didn't want to push too much and make for an awkward moment. I must say Robert was one of the friendliest and kindest strangers I have ever met.

We all said our final good-byes and bid them both a safe journey. I remember watching after them for a few moments and thinking they could just fly up into the sky and ride the clouds. There was something out of this world about this encounter. My heart, mind and soul had taken flight high above the clouds and beyond. I didn't want to come back down.

67

Desktop Image & Likeness

The children and I went back into the house. I requested they wash their hands, get out their lunches and come to the kitchen table. While they were doing this, I happened to glance over in the direction of my computer monitor and focused on the desktop image. It was an artist's beautiful rendering of Jesus that I had found on the internet the previous year. I recall searching for an inspiring image to put on my screen and was immediately drawn to this one. As I was studying the image on my computer screen I thought there was something about it that reminded me of Robert—the mouth, the face shape, the hair, the eyes, the countenance—the whole impression was familiar in some way. I filed these thoughts in the back of my mind and proceeded with the needs of the present moment.

68

I've Got Land

While the children were eating their lunch we discussed what had happened earlier. A couple of them thought that what had happened was "really cool." They had enjoyed the songs presented by Robert and Elijah and appreciated the personal words and thoughtful gifts from Robert. This is when the oldest girl shared that when Robert had asked her to hug him "like I am your father" that she felt consoled, as that very morning she had been missing her father who lived in another country. A couple of the children confirmed that Robert had mentioned the land in Nova Scotia on the walk. One of the children thought they were from Heaven. They were all at peace about our visitors and with childlike innocence were open to the impossible becoming possible.

I let them know that I would mention what had happened later in the day to their parents and that they could further discuss it with them. I did send an email to the parents that evening explaining what had transpired and the gift of music and encouragement the children were given. I only heard back from one parent who was a bit concerned because they were strangers. I reassured her the children were watched closely by me and that all went well. I told her I thought it was something Heaven-sent but I wouldn't know for sure until I got to Heaven. I didn't feel a need to try to convince her and she wasn't obligated to believe. It is often difficult to explain an event to a person who wasn't there, especially if it is something spiritual. I believe we were truly blessed that special summer day.

69

Comical

After lunch we had some quiet reading time. The children either brought their own books from home or selected one from my small home library. This was a beautiful time for the children to relax with their favourite books or to discover something new. I cleaned up the kitchen while they read, then prepared for the next activity.

At one point, my daughter came rushing to the kitchen with one of her friends while holding a book. She was so excited to share with me that the book her friend had brought that day was filled with red roses. I took the book and flipped through the pages, noting several of the pages had illustrated bouquets of red roses. My daughter reminded me of the St. Thérèse of Lisieux Novena prayer she and her brother had just finished the day before, which promised to let fall a shower of roses. Could this be the sign that our prayer had been heard? I realize it was both my daughter and my oldest son who had prayed the Novena together with the same intention. Perhaps this was the sign for my daughter that her prayer had been answered. Maybe it was meant for my son too as he always enjoyed watching cartoons growing up and this was a children's graphic novel. God has a sense of humour and if

He chooses through His beloved daughter St. Thérèse to shower us with cartoon red roses, then why not?

There was also the real rose bush on the walk that we were all invited to observe by Robert. It was a double blessing of roses!

70

Verification

Since I knew that Robert had gone to visit the workers next door during his visit with us, I decided to check in with them and see what had transpired. After breakfast the following day, I went outside and around the corner of my building to see if I could see any of the men working on the building next door. I quickly saw two people and went to talk with the older man.

I greeted him and then asked if someone named Robert had come over to talk with them yesterday. The worker affirmed this by telling me that yes, he had stopped to talk with them. I then asked what Robert had said. The worker told me that Robert had mentioned land that he had in Nova Scotia. There it was again, for the third or fourth time; the land in Nova Scotia.

What was it about that land that Robert kept repeating, first at the church, then to the children, then to me, and finally to the workers?

71

Cleaning Companion

The Sunbeams summer program finished. My daughter began another year at the "little school with the big heart." I began to work part-time in the office at DMCS and continued with my Sunbeams After-school program.

To help pay for our daughter's tuition, my husband and I cleaned the school a couple of times during the week and on weekends. We were so grateful to have this opportunity to help pay our daughter's tuition. Parents make sacrifices for their children and this was one we were willing to do for her as she was thriving at this school. The cleaning was a bit challenging for us both. We got a system in place and pushed ahead to get the cleaning completed well.

There were times I would go to the school to clean and would visit the chapel to ask Jesus to help me. Then about halfway through my cleaning shift when I was exhausted and still had more cleaning ahead, I would return to the chapel with more prayers asking for more grace to complete the job. He was always there to help me through. I then began to offer the cleaning for different intentions including those in my family and the world. No work is ever wasted and it can all be offered to God for His higher purposes.

This job gave me more appreciation for all who clean. It is hard, physical work and not easy for most people. Whenever you walk into a clean home, office, school, or building, remember someone had to work very hard to clean it! Appreciate it, be grateful, be thankful!

72

What's In a Name

Partway through the school year, I was cuddling with my daughter on a small couch in our kitchen. The visit from Robert and Elijah came to mind and I realized that "later this year" had come and gone without any contact from Robert. The other time parameter he had mentioned was "next summer" and we were now in the next year. Meeting Robert and Elijah the previous summer had left me with a wonder at all that had transpired, and with a glimmer of hope that there was more to be revealed in the future.

I began to think about the two names and if there was any special significance to them. I decided to look up both names' meanings online. I searched for the meaning of Robert first. I silently read the meaning and cross-referenced with a few different websites. The meanings of Robert included: bright, famous, shining, bright-fame, glory-bright, and shining with glory. I was amazed at the meanings that came up.

Next I searched for the meaning of Elijah. The searches yielded the following results: Yahweh is my God, Jehovah is my God.

Elijah was a prophet in the Old Testament who saved the Jewish people from worshipping a false god. Elijah prayed to God, asking for a miracle to show He was the true God. His prayer was answered in a powerful way, which turned back the hearts of the people to the real God. You can read about it in these Bible scriptures: 1 Kings 18. Here is an excerpt:

> At the time of the offering of the oblation, the prophet Elijah came near and said, 'O Lord, God of Abraham, Isaac, and Israel, let it be known this day that you are God in Israel, that I am your servant, and that I have done all these things at your bidding. Answer me, O Lord, answer me, so that this people may know that you, O Lord, are God, and that you have turned their hearts back.' Then the fire of the Lord fell and consumed the burnt offering, the wood, the stones, and the dust, and even licked up the water that was in the trench. When all the people saw it, they fell on their faces and said, 'The Lord indeed is God; the Lord indeed is God.'
> (1 Kings 18:36-39)

The spiritual significance of both names' meanings was profound. I once again filed it away in my mind and *pondered them in my heart*.

73

Beauty So Ancient

A group of interested people in the area had petitioned our bishop for a Traditional Latin Mass (TLM) to be held in our diocese and it was approved. A recently ordained priest was willing to learn this Mass, and with much support the plans moved ahead. The *resurrected* Traditional Latin Mass was celebrated for the first time in 50 years in Saint John at Holy Trinity Catholic Church.

Some had attended a TLM at this same church or elsewhere when they were growing up or as younger adults, while for others it was the first time. I myself had a distant memory of attending Mass at the Cathedral of the Immaculate Conception as a very young child. I do recall not understanding what was being said as it was in Latin and I was too young to read the Mass book, or missal. I did know, even at a young age, that there was something special happening in the church, but wouldn't understand its significance for many more years.

The Traditional Latin Mass, often called the Mass of the Ages, was the Mass celebrated all over the world for over 1500 years. A Catholic could attend the Mass at a church anywhere in the world and understand what was happening as they would have come to know the Latin.

There were also Mass booklets or missals that had Latin on one side of the page and one's local language on the other so it was easy to follow along no matter where you were attending.

This Traditional Latin Mass that I was now attending, also known as the Tridentine Mass, followed the Traditional Rite, which was in place since 1570 until 1962 throughout most of the world, building upon previous Mass rites going back to the early Church. During the 1960s a new form of the Mass emerged after the well-known Vatican II Council met. These changes were voted on with the majority deciding to update or modernize the Mass, which became known as the Novus Ordo (New Order) Mass. Not everyone agreed with the changes and for various reasons continued attending the Traditional Latin Mass, with some driving considerable distances each Sunday to attend. Unfortunately for some dioceses the TLM diminished or stopped completely. But in many parts of the world the Traditional Latin Mass continued uninterrupted.

Attending the Traditional Latin Mass as an adult for the first time was an exceptional experience. I was drawn in by its beauty, its reverence, the unchanging Latin, the priest turning away from the congregation and towards God, the smell of incense, the chime of bells, the hymns from long ago, and the many moments of silence. Everyone receiving Communion kneeling and on the tongue is another way of honouring our Lord Jesus truly present in the Eucharistic Host. This ancient rite had helped to make saints out of sinners for hundreds of years. It was timeless—a link between the past and present. This encounter with *beauty so ancient* (and yet so new) deepened my love for the Mass and my love for Jesus, who, with the priest's words of Consecration, came once again to join with His people in Communion, bringing His love and grace.

Many young adults are discovering the Traditional Latin Mass for the first time and are being drawn to it. They cherish all that makes this Mass so different from what they are used to. They want to protect it for their children and future generations. If this ancient Mass will draw more people to the Church, and many are preferring it, then all the more reason not to reduce it or eliminate it. Not everyone will prefer the TLM, but I encourage everyone to consider attending a TLM for a couple of months with an open mind and heart. You may discover its timeless beauty too or at least understand a little more why others do.

I do not have a preference between the Traditional Latin Mass or the Novus Ordo and attend both where possible. But I do see the value of keeping the TLM intact as there is something so beautiful and unique about this Mass of the Ages that is not easily found in the Novus Ordo Masses. I do not want to see the Traditional Latin Mass disappear as it connects us with the past, brings the past to the present, and the present to our future: our great hope to be forever united with our Lord Jesus Christ in Heaven. It is important that the Church not think it has to reduce, restrict, or eliminate this beautiful form of worship. It is a rare gem that needs to be protected. I have attended both forms of the Masses and as long as the teachings align with the Bible and the Magisterium of the Church (teaching authority which Christ has given to the Church, those who exercise this authority, and the teachings of faith) and there is a reverence amongst those in attendance for the great Miracle of Love happening, I think both can co-exist peacefully. One does not need to replace the other. We are all made differently and have different ways of worshipping. Most importantly, Jesus is present at both and He loves us all.

74

Foot Taxi

In addition to attending the monthly TLM at Holy Trinity Catholic Church, we began to attend the weekly Novus Ordo Sunday Mass there. The same priest offered both Masses and we began to appreciate and enjoy this community. There was weekly Catechism for the children, programs for adults, church potlucks and new friendships.

I recall in the weeks prior to Easter the priest announcing a call for volunteers to have their feet washed during the Holy Thursday Mass. This was a symbolic gesture of what Jesus did for His disciples on the night before he died, and an example for us all. Since it was something that Jesus had done for his male disciples, I had never volunteered, thinking it best to leave it for the men to represent the disciples.

The next Sunday, the priest announced once more that there were still spots available for the foot washing. I felt a little nudge about volunteering, but then dismissed it, thinking others would step up. The following and final Sunday before Holy Thursday, the priest announced the need for two more volunteers. I felt a strong prodding that I should volunteer, along with my daughter. I decided to wait until after Mass and check the sign-up sheet before leaving. If the spots were still available I would sign-up. Sure enough when I went to check the sheet, there were still two spots left. I knew somehow that I was meant to volunteer, along with my daughter. Sometimes we can be too restrictive in our thinking and miss the important message Jesus wants us to understand. I was learning to trust this still small voice more, knowing God was leading me for His purposes.

Holy Thursday arrived and I made sure we were showered and our feet were especially clean! My husband would not be attending as he was away visiting his sick father. I was planning to walk to the church which was about thirty minutes away but thought the walk would not keep my feet clean or fresh. Also, I didn't want to arrive at the church tired, out of breath, and too warm after the long walk. I thought the best option was to call a cab, leaving plenty of extra time so we would be ready to partake in this small but important gesture in honour of our Lord.

The cab driver arrived to pick us up and away we went to the church. Always mindful that the people around me might need to hear some Good News, I started talking about why I was going to the church. The cab driver quickly responded to what I was saying and shared some of his faith journey with me including how he had suffered for a long time living in a war-torn country and had developed PTSD. He told me he started attending a prayer group at Stella Maris Catholic Church—one I had heard about but hadn't attended yet, at least not as an adult. He shared that someone who attended this prayer group suggested the Sacrament of Confession to him, giving him hope that Jesus could help him to heal from PTSD. Not being Catholic but another close faith, he decided to go to Confession which is known as a healing Sacrament. He told me Jesus healed him of PTSD! I was so honoured to hear his powerful testimony.

He was interested in my conversion story so I quickly told him as we were almost at the church. He then invited me to the prayer group and offered to give me a drive if I needed one. He also mentioned something about a summer conference that had a special presenter who had gifts of healing. I had never heard of the conference before but it piqued my interest. He gave me his taxi number and we said our goodbyes with great peace knowing we had shared the Good News with each other.

The Holy Thursday Mass was beautiful and both my daughter and I, along with the other volunteers, had our feet (or rather *one* of our feet to save time) washed by the priest, as a remembrance of what Jesus had done so long ago. It was a simple, humble, compassionate gesture—in honour of our Saviour and still relevant to this day.

> After he had washed their feet, had put on his robe, and had returned to the table, he said to them, "Do you know what I have done to you? You call me Teacher and Lord—and you are right, for that is what I am. So if I, your Lord and Teacher, have washed your feet, you also ought to wash one another's feet. For I have set you an example, that you also should do as I have done to you. Very truly, I tell you, servants are not greater than their master, nor are messengers greater than the one who sent them. If you know these things, you are blessed if you do them. (John 13:12-17)

75

Conference Buzz

The following week I called my taxi friend to ask for a drive to the prayer group at Stella Maris Catholic Church and he generously agreed. He told me his conversion story in more detail on the way and I was amazed at all he had overcome and the healing Jesus had given him. The prayer group was warm and welcoming, the music uplifting, the Bible reading inspiring, and the witnessing and sharing encouraging.

The atmosphere was powerfully transformed with the presence of God. It says in the Bible that God inhabits our praises. I definitely could feel His presence in the room. It was filled with peace, love, joy, holiness…a bit of Heaven come down to be with us. Afterwards there was some fellowship and a snack table. I chatted with some of the people and the repeating theme was about this upcoming conference. I was beginning to have a deep desire to go but not sure how I would be able to get there nor how to pay for it.

I continued to attend the prayer group at Stella Maris Catholic Church weekly and I became friends with a kind older lady who was able to drive me, as my taxi friend was not always available due to his work. I was so thankful for her generosity in driving me and her kind and thoughtful ways. She and the others I met at this prayer group were a reminder of what people walking closely with Jesus are like. This beautiful community of believers gave me a glimpse of what our life in Heaven will be like: a truly warm, caring, and welcoming place where all are well-loved, accepted, and cherished.

The Queen of Peace prayer group that I had originally attended at St. Peter's Catholic Church had disbanded and a new prayer group had begun there with a new leader. I attended this prayer group a few times too and once again kept hearing about the summer conference and how amazing it was. I was given a pamphlet about it and once again my desire to go deepened. I prayed about it when I got home, asking God to make a way so that I could attend.

76

Bible Drive

I was inspired to organize a middle school mission project for my daughter and a few other students from her school. We decided to volunteer at a local thrift store that uses the money they raise to fund missions throughout the world. The girls sorted donations, put stock out, organized displays, and greeted and served customers. It was a great learning experience for them.

While supervising the girls, I noticed they had a book section with an extensive selection of Bibles and other spiritual books. There was a volunteer who managed it and I began to discuss with him how I often would share the Good News with people I met. With his help and the support of the manager, I was able to get a good stack of Bibles to distribute.

I had previously checked into the cost of ordering Bibles and they were at least $50 per case of Bibles. I didn't have that extra money and so I was so grateful for these donations of Bibles. They were also able to give me some of their new Bibles that they use for their missions. You don't have to go overseas to find a mission field; there is already one in our midst. I gave out the Bibles when the opportunity presented itself and soon I needed more.

I decided to have a Bible drive, where I would request donations of new or nearly new Bibles from the churches in my diocese. I created flyers and with the help of a few friends, got the message out. We put boxes in the entrances of several churches for the month of April. The people's response to the drive was overwhelming. By the month's end I had many boxes of beautiful Bibles to share with others. I was able to store them at DMCS and had a priest bless them all. I would take a bag of the donated Bibles home with me to distribute when I got the chance. But there were still so many to give out; a happy problem to have! I was wondering how I was going to get all of the Bibles handed out in a timely way.

One night there was a knock on my door and I looked out to see a short, stout woman asking for donations of bottles. I opened the door and gave her the few bottles I had. As we chatted, she looked past me and noticed the bags filled with Bibles. She asked me if they were Bibles and I confirmed they were. There were a few bags of Bibles I had carted home from the school with intentions to hand them out one by one. I explained to her what I had done and that I was a bit overwhelmed by the success of the Bible Drive, and with a busy life as most of us have, I was concerned about it taking a long time to distribute them.

She wasted no time and responded with enthusiasm saying she could hand some out. I couldn't believe that here in front of me was the answer to my prayers. I sensed in her humble simplicity a pure heart and so I gave her a bag of Bibles to share with others, thinking I might see her again another day. Off she went into the evening with the Bibles, and soon there was another knock on my door. She had returned with an empty bag. I was astonished. "You gave these Bibles out already?" I asked incredulously. She began to list how and to whom she gave them. She then told me she could take another bag to distribute and so I gave her another bag. Out she went again and a short while later she returned. Off with a third bag she went again, but I told her that was the limit for the day as it was getting late. I also told her she could wait until the next day to hand them out or whenever was convenient for her. Her determination was so inspiring. She loved the Lord and she was so happy to have this opportunity to serve Him. She was truly a blessing and I believe God sent her to help me.

I distributed many of the Bibles too, along with some other friends. Sometimes I brought them with me to the Rosary Rallies and there was often someone new who would join us and receive one of the Bibles with much appreciation. Somehow, even though in our society not as many people attend church, there is still a respect and honour of this Great Book and most people appreciate receiving one.

I do recall one day handing some Bibles out in my neighbourhood. I gave one to an older gentleman who graciously received it. Nearby was a young boy about ten years old. He was curious about what I was handing out and asked about it. To simplify, I told him it was a book about Jesus. I then asked him if he knew about Jesus. He shook his head and asked, "Who is Jesus?" I instantly felt a pang of sorrow and deep compassion for this young, curious boy. I felt a bit sad to think so many children are being raised without the knowledge of God and His great plan of Salvation. I quickly gave the boy a brief description of who Jesus is, what He did for us, and also mentioned Heaven, and what the Bible was. He earnestly accepted a Bible and then he asked if he could have another one for his brother. I was so touched by his humility and innocence, that at that moment I just could not say "one per family" or any other limitation. I thought how beautiful it would be if the brothers explored the Bible together. I gave him an additional Bible and prayed later that Jesus would bless him and his family.

When I was growing up, I heard the name of Jesus spoken so often including in the public sphere that it was common knowledge that

Jesus was our Saviour. But slowly His name has been spoken less and less and the knowledge of who He is has been reduced, often purposely silenced. We need to make His name known everywhere again! Every soul needs to hear the Good News!

77

The Call

One evening in early July, I received a call from a woman I knew through church circles and who sometimes attended the Rosary Rallies and prayer groups. She was such a kind-hearted woman, about fifteen years older than me. I had met her shortly after my reversion many years before and noticed she had a great light and joy about her. She was light-hearted and funny and you always felt accepted and supported by her. I didn't know her really well but I knew she loved the Lord.

During the telephone conversation, she told me that she had been planning to attend the summer conference but was unable to due to having to take care of her cats who didn't do well when she was away. She had prayed about who she should give her already paid-for ticket to and my name was the first one that came into her mind after she prayed. I could hardly believe it! This was an answer to my prayer! She did not want any money for it and was happy to gift it to me so that I could go. I told her I had a great desire to go and had prayed asking God to make a way. He answered my prayer and He made a way! My friend also let me know that the whole weekend, including food and accommodations, was included. I would be sharing adjoining rooms with another woman I knew from one of the prayer groups and would travel with her. Everything was taken care of. I thanked my friend and let her know God had blessed me through her.

Ask, Seek, Knock
"Ask and it will be given to you; seek and you will find; knock and the door will be opened to you. (Matthew 7:7)

78

Conference Weekend

The conference was held in August and I travelled with the friend who I would be sharing the adjoining space with, along with two other women who were also attending the conference. The conference was being held at Mount Allison University in Sackville, New Brunswick and was sponsored by the Atlantic Service Committee Catholic Charismatic Renewal.

We checked in to receive our conference pass and keys to our rooms. We went to our rooms to get settled in and my friend and I agreed on a time to meet to go to the dining hall. We ate supper with many of the conference attendees and then headed to the auditorium for the opening of the conference.

The MC of the conference began with welcoming us and opening with prayer. He introduced the various ministry teams and gave a little overview of each. The music ministry was present on the right side of the stage. They would lead praise and worship at various times throughout the conference weekend. On the other side was a group who had various gifts including gifts of knowledge and healing.

He then introduced the main guest speaker for the conference who came from California. This man has gifts of healing, leads a ministry in his home state, travels to present at conferences throughout various parts of the world, and is a published author. We also discovered he was kind, compassionate, funny, wise, and serious about teaching on various important topics to help deepen our faith. He would be leading the sessions during the weekend.

I was so grateful and excited to be here with other believers desiring to draw closer to our King and Saviour Jesus Christ! There was no other place on earth I wanted to be than here at this life-changing conference!

The praise and worship band began to play beautiful music and the lead singer drew the crowd in with her uplifting voice. They had the lyrics to the songs on a big screen so we could all join in. Soon I was lifted up into the Spirit and felt such peace and joy while worshipping God with so many others.

Next was the Eucharist of Thanksgiving, the Mass. We were all so blessed to receive Jesus this evening and to be in Communion with our God and each other.

There was a man who would occasionally share a Word of Knowledge with the audience. At other times, some of the other members of the ministry teams would come to the centre podium to share messages they were receiving from God. I was amazed to hear these words spoken to us through these vessels of God. The words were always filled with truth and love and left me with great peace and gratitude.

The final part of the evening was Adoration where the Blessed Sacrament of the Holy Eucharist was exposed in the special holder called the Monstrance for us all to adore. This is another way to draw close to Jesus as He pours out His love and grace upon us.

At the end of the evening we returned to our rooms and I quickly fell asleep filled with a most amazing peace, knowing I had a full day ahead to continue to draw closer to my Lord.

79

Spoken Over Me

The next morning we enjoyed a delicious breakfast then headed to the conference auditorium. The day was a busy one filled with prayer, praise and worship, the guest speaker's teachings, and more Words of Knowledge. We had short breaks as well as a delicious lunch. There were priests available to hear Confessions and so I waited patiently in a long line to confess my sins to Jesus working through the priest. Jesus is truly present in the Sacrament of Confession and it is He who forgives, using the priest as a conduit of grace. I know how I feel before Confession and then afterwards—it is real and I am thankful for His mercy and forgiveness.

In the afternoon there was a special teaching from the main guest speaker on healing and then he invited people to come up to ask for healings in various parts of their bodies, as well as mental and emotional healings. The healing ministry team was also available with their gifts to share. Many people in attendance went up with various ailments and returned to their seats with healing. It was powerful to witness these miraculous healings for those who had suffered for so long.

At one point he mentioned that someone shared that they had seen Jesus riding on a donkey in the auditorium. Why on a donkey? This was one way that we would know that Jesus was truly present with us, as he rode on a lowly donkey when he lived here on the earth two thousand years ago.

We had a delicious dinner in the dining hall and returned to the auditorium for the evening session. Once again there was beautiful praise and worship music and one of the presenters announced that some ministry members were going to go amongst us in the auditorium and bring us Words of Knowledge as the Holy Spirit led them. I recall thinking that it would be interesting to receive a word from God through his ministers, but I didn't hold out that I would be one of the chosen. God can choose whomever He wants to receive a message and so I continued to praise Jesus with abandon and peace while several people weaved through the auditorium imparting their heavenly messages.

All of a sudden I was aware of someone coming into my aisle of seats. I could see them out of my peripheral vision, and so I was moving forward to let them pass by me to get to their seat. But they were not passing me by. They were there to deliver a message to me. I began to hear these words from the woman God had directed to me, "My daughter, I am well pleased. Thank you for bringing so many souls to me." I immediately began to tear up as I knew these were truly words from God. I could hardly believe I was being blessed in this way. But I humbly received these words and my heart leapt for joy! There were a few more words that I don't recall now but the main message was so incredible to hear. You see, if I had received this message ten years before, it would not have made sense to me. But over the past few years I had been sharing the Good News with many people I met especially strangers—on the street, in parks and other gatherings. God was thanking me for bringing Him souls. My God was recognizing my service to Him and my brothers and sisters. My mostly hidden work for the Lord had not gone unnoticed by the One I desired to serve.

There was once again the Eucharist of Thanksgiving, followed by Adoration. The music ministry filled the room with inspiring music that lifted us closer to Heaven. The main guest speaker invited more of us to come on the stage to ask for healing. Whether physical, mental, emotional, or spiritual, there were many healings and especially a healing of our hearts—we all knew we were loved by our Saviour Jesus.

The next day was the final half-day of the conference. It went quickly with prayer, praise, and the closing Eucharist of Thanksgiving. I departed that day with my soul renewed and refreshed, ready to re-enter the world once again. This time I would be bringing the Good News with the added extraordinary gifts of grace I received on this unforgettable weekend.

> For no prophecy was ever produced by the will of man, but men spoke from God as they were carried along by the Holy Spirit. (2 Peter 1:21)

80

AGM Invite

On the way back from the summer conference my friend that I was travelling with mentioned to me that there was going to be an Annual General Meeting (AGM) for the Between The Hearts Renewal Centre, near Amherst, Nova Scotia, not far from the New Brunswick border. I knew an acquaintance who was involved with this centre and I had heard good things about what they were doing. It was a retreat centre that was situated centrally for access from New Brunswick, Nova Scotia, and Prince Edward Island. (Maybe Newfoundland too!) They had conferences, retreats, workshops, and other faith-based events. I asked a few more questions about it and she told me it was like a mini summer conference as they would have prayer, praise music, Mass—similar to what we had just experienced. There would be the AGM meeting component too and I would be welcome to provide my input.

It all sounded interesting and I was definitely curious. I don't think I needed any convincing and I think by the time I got home, I was certain I would be attending the AGM at the end of October. I would once again travel with my friend and the costs were affordable as I would be sharing a room and we would also have some inhouse potluck meals to keep the costs down. It was a couple of months away but I booked it off as somehow I knew I was meant to be there.

81

Retreating Once Again

The two months went by quickly and I was once again travelling with my friend to the long-awaited AGM, which was a mix of mini-conference, retreat, and meetings. A couple of other women travelled with us and we enjoyed interesting conversations along the way, mostly about our shared faith.

When I arrived I checked in and got settled in my room. We had stopped at a restaurant along the way for supper so we were ready for the evening. The AGM started with a welcome and introductions by the Executive Director who shared the AGM weekend plans. We followed with communal prayer and then a man I recognized from the summer conference began singing and playing his guitar. A few others sang with him and soon many more joined in. Once again, we brought God in our midst and we were filled with His peace, love, and joy.

After singing a few songs, I decided to go to sleep early wanting to make the most of the next day. Falling asleep after worshipping the Lord is like sleeping on a cloud. I quickly fell asleep and floated into my dreams.

82

A Meeting Like No Other

The following day we all joined together for breakfast in the common area. There were so many kind and welcoming people there. They were truly showing the hospitality of Jesus. I felt like I belonged among these people. It felt like home and I was once again so grateful to be here.

The AGM began after breakfast with prayer, some praise and then the meeting itinerary. The day was broken into several meeting sessions. I listened intently to all that was being planned and offered my input where possible and effective. I was a newbie after all but sometimes an outsider may have insights that can provide a new or refreshing perspective. Between the meeting sessions there were prayers, Bible scripture readings, reflections, praise, delicious food, and warm fellowship. I recognized some familiar faces from the summer conference and as we were all here for a common purpose—the furthering of the Kingdom, we were of one accord, abiding in Him.

In particular, I noticed a man here who was from the summer conference. He had sometimes offered Words of Knowledge to the whole group at the conference. I was so happy to see him here once more. He was an older man, who looked to be in his late sixties, and seemed to be filled with God's peace and wisdom. I noticed that people would approach him during breaks and he would impart a few beautiful words to them. I was in the kitchen and heard him sharing his gift with someone and I couldn't help but overhear. I was wondering if there might be a word for me, so I summoned the courage to ask him. He quickly imparted a few inspiring words to me that were edifying to my heart, mind, and soul.

We broke for lunch and once again the same gentleman was sharing his gift with others who approached him. I was bold enough to ask again and he once more gave me another beautiful encouraging word—or it was really the Lord who gave the words to me through His vessel. This was like no other AGM I had ever attended when I served in the volunteer sector. This life in the Spirit was where I preferred to be and I wanted more of it.

83

Divine Mercy

We went out for supper and then reconvened for an evening of prayer, praise, and fellowship. After the busy but fulfilling day, I was looking forward to focusing on God alone (God the Father, God the Son–Jesus, and God the Holy Spirit—three Divine Persons in One God.)

The small group of singers and guitar players began to lead us in praising God. As I sang along, I glanced across the room and noticed a framed image of Divine Mercy on a beautiful gold stand. This is the image that Saint Faustina was asked to have painted after Jesus appeared to her and gave her messages to share with the world about His Divine Mercy. The first rendering of the image by an artist was not satisfactory to Saint Faustina and so there was another one painted. I am not sure how many were painted until the essence of Jesus' appearance was captured but I do know this was a copy of one of them. I had seen this particular rendition in churches in my city as well as at the school my daughter attended. It was my favourite rendition.

I kept glancing over at the Divine Mercy image and as if I were drawn to it, I got up from my seat and moved closer to the image. I peered at it with interest and wonder. I remember thinking there was a familiarity about this image. I studied the face and then it clicked. There was a similarity between this image and the one I had on my computer as a desktop image. This image too reminded me of meeting Robert, the day he came to my house. The eyes, the face shape, the mouth, the hair, the eyes, the essence were all familiar to me. I was deeply stirred in my spirit and, almost moved to tears, quickly left the room.

84

Quiet Time

I began walking through the centre, trying to hold back the tears but feeling like I was going to burst. After worshipping God through the powerful music, and gazing upon the Divine Mercy picture, I wanted to go somewhere to be alone. I went through a large meeting space and noticed signs for the chapel. The door was open and I walked into a small, quiet space. I quickly closed the door, knelt down and cried out to Jesus. "Jesus, what do you want with me?" The tears flowed as I was left alone with my Saviour. I poured out my heart to Him, asking Him to let me know what He wanted me to do. I was confused and not sure what my next steps were. After my fountain of tears and questions subsided, I was left as a child being comforted by my Father. I found a Bible and read some scriptures. I prayed the Rosary. I sat in stillness, in peace, in Love.

85

May I Have a Word From You?

After a refreshing sleep, I once more gathered with the group for breakfast. There was a buzz amongst everyone, as we knew there were only a few hours remaining of the AGM, and most importantly, the gathering together in friendship with Christ.

I noticed once more that the man with the Gift of Knowledge was being approached by others to receive a Word of Knowledge. I was a bit shy and nervous to approach him again and kept hesitating. Once when I was in the kitchen getting something I overheard him giving a message to someone else and so I once more boldly summoned the courage to ask if he had a word for me. He looked at me intently and within seconds words came flowing through him to me as a gift from Heaven. They were beautiful, encouraging words that lifted my spirit. I thanked him and carried the words with me throughout the morning.

We had prayer and praise and a final meeting session. When we had a mid-morning break, once more this man was sharing his gift with others. With his gift of Words of Knowledge I wondered if he might have some insight into what had happened the day I met Robert. I thought to myself, "What do I have to lose?" I took a deep breath and proceeded to ask him if he might be willing to give me some feedback on something that happened to me. He quickly agreed and so I began to recount the story of the day I met Robert and Elijah.

He listened closely and I gave as much detail as I could while being mindful of his time and the break we were on. I then finished my sharing of that memorable day and waited for his response.

86

Do You Want to Know?

He looked intently at me and then he asked, "Do you want to know who that was?"

I quickly responded, "Yes!"

He then announced, "That was Jesus."

I replied, "I thought it might be but wasn't sure."

He then said, "And the person with him, that was Saint Michael the Archangel. Saint Michael always goes before Jesus."

And just like that we confirmed and believed together that the unexpected visitors I met and invited to my house that day were Jesus Christ and Saint Michael. I had thought it might be Jesus and possibly an angel, but now I had it confirmed. It was the best Word of Knowledge I received that day. I finally had closure about that unusual summer day; that it was King Jesus who came to visit us, along with St. Michael, Prince of the Heavenly Army! I was awestruck at this revelation!

87

Floating on a Cloud

After the break, the final meeting session resumed. I tried my best to be present with the group but I felt like I was floating on a cloud. This was a cloud so high it could touch Heaven, knowing my Saviour and his right-hand angel had come to visit us. I was astonished at all that had transpired since that summer day and the special arranging of people, events, and gifts that led me to the present. It started as a simple meeting with strangers, a coffee invitation, and a promise for the future. Now that everything had been verified, I finally had closure, and peace, but I would never be the same again, nor would I want to be.

88

Keep Writing

The AGM wrapped up with prayer and then we had a priest come and offer the Holy Sacrifice of the Mass in the larger room outside the small chapel as there wasn't enough space in the chapel. It was such a special Mass to me as I acknowledged and thanked my God for his Great Gift.

Afterwards, as we were all packing up and getting ready to depart, I once again observed the man with the Gift of Knowledge communicating messages of hope and love from Heaven to those who asked. Even though he had confirmed my deepest hope in our previous conversation, there were a couple of other questions and concerns I had that he might be able to offer some insights from Heaven on.

I approached him for the final time and asked him if he might have a Word of Knowledge on a book I was writing. I told him I had been given a book as though a divine download and was writing it but was unsure whether I was to continue. He looked directly at me and said, "Keep writing. The world needs that book." That was another confirmation that gave me relief and peace. I have since wondered if this also applies to any and all books that I have written or will write, including the first book I previously published in 2021, and now this second one that you are reading. The third book I plan to finish writing next and to publish is the divine downloaded book. I also have plans to write a fourth, a fifth and maybe more books. I will see how the Lord leads me in the coming months and years.

The final question I had was about my family. I asked him about my husband and my grown sons. Like most mothers and wives, I am concerned about the well-being and Eternal destination of those I love. Without hesitation he replied, "Pray for them." It was one simple Word of Knowledge but it was the best one, the strongest one, the most powerful answer for my concerns. It was given from Heaven and it was enough. Once again, I was at peace. The power of prayer was unchanging. I would continue with hope, peace, and love to pray for those near and far that they would all be found in God's Kingdom of Love one day.

89

Rabbit or Hare?

On the way home, I shared what had happened with my friend who was driving and her other guest who was driving back with us. My friend never doubted the events I shared with her about Robert and Elijah, that the man with the Gift of Knowledge had confirmed. She immediately believed that this had truly happened to me. I don't need to have anyone believe me but it is comforting to know there are others by your side who do believe and are open to miracles from Heaven.

We had decided to go apple picking on the way back home. To get there we took a scenic route past Sackville, New Brunswick and drove through a quaint town called Memramcook. As we were driving through the town, we went past a restaurant and my friend called out the name, LeBlanc, and she mentioned that they had delicious food. I quickly looked at the time and it was after 1:00 pm so I asked if she wanted to have lunch there. She agreed as did our other passenger so she slowed down, turned around, and drove back to the restaurant.

As we were walking up to the front door of the restaurant, I noticed some statues in a garden to the left of the door. I moved in to take a closer look at them and spotted an additional statue in the corner of the garden that I hadn't seen from the walkway. I observed this one was holding something. I moved in closer and realized it was a woman who looked like a saint or angel holding a rabbit, or hare.

It seemed unusual at first but then I thought about all that had happened over the weekend and thought *yes*, this fits right in. My daughter had been given a rabbit by a family friend to try out. They were unable to keep the rabbit for several reasons and so were looking for a home for it. My daughter was trying out taking care of the rabbit for a few weeks to see if she was capable of and interested in keeping it as a pet. She was doing well and really enjoyed being with the sweet rabbit. I had told her that we would decide by October 31 if she was to keep it, based on how well she was taking care of the rabbit up to that point. When I saw this statue of the woman holding the rabbit on the last day of the month of October, I took this as the sign that *yes*, my daughter was to keep the rabbit as her pet.

The statue reminded me of the story of Saint Melangell, the patron saint of hares and rabbits. I had learned about this special saint from friends who took care of rabbits. Legend has it that Saint Melangell was the daughter of an Irish king who wanted her to marry a nobleman. Melangell, who had taken a vow of celibacy, fled to the countryside, and lived as a hermitess for many years. A prince was hare hunting one day with his hunting dogs, and the hare ran to Melangell and hid under her robe. When the prince and his dogs caught up to the location of the hare, he met Melangell and learned of her story. He was moved to give her and God a parcel of land to be a sanctuary for all who fled there. She had an abbey built on the land and became the abbess. She died in 590.

When I returned home and shared the story and decision with my daughter, she was overjoyed both with the unique story and the good news that she would be a sanctuary for her own rabbit. I was happy for her and reassured that the right decision had been made with the hidden sign made visible with help from Heaven!

90

He Delights In Us

God is truly in the details of life and He delights in surprising His children with good things that will enrich and satisfy them in a deep and meaningful way. He is the Great Creator and Storyteller and has made each one of us a part of His Story—history!

Why did Jesus decide to visit me on this one particular day? I do believe it was in answer to the Novena prayer that my daughter and son were praying together. I had also said a few prayers on my own during this Novena. Heaven hears each and every one of our prayers and always answers them. Sometimes it is a yes, sometimes it is a no, and sometimes it is a "not right now but at the perfect time," as God is arranging the circumstances for something better for us. Where does our Novena prayer fit in with this? I believe it was answered with a "yes" in an incredibly unique way—in a grace-filled, supernatural way. We were praying with expectant faith and God did not disappoint!

Although my son never came up to the kitchen to meet our visitors, he did still hear about what happened later. He tried to make sense of what happened but did not cross over into the spiritual realm of possibility that this was an answer to the Novena he had prayed with his sister. To think he was just seconds and steps from meeting Jesus but missed this Divine Appointment is disappointing, but when I looked over at Jesus in my kitchen that day, He knew my son was seconds and steps from Him too. But Jesus does not push. He invites, He draws, He beckons. He waits for our response. Love is patient.

I will continue to pray for my oldest son's Salvation. If you are reading this and could spare a prayer, please pray that my son will come to believe in Jesus and be taken to Heaven for Eternity in God's perfect time. Also please pray for my other son, a few years younger and living in another province, that he will come back to Jesus and be truly saved and live in Heaven for Eternity too. I have become a beggar for souls, especially for the souls of my children, husband, family, and relatives. All souls are precious in God's sight. He created each one and He wants them to return to His Kingdom in Heaven. He is a Good Father. Our Father!

> **Instructions Concerning Prayer**
> First of all, then, I urge that supplications, prayers, intercessions, and thanksgivings be made for everyone, for kings and all who are in high positions, so that we may lead a quiet and peaceable life in all godliness and dignity. This is right and is acceptable in the sight of God our Saviour, who desires everyone to be saved and to come to the knowledge of the truth. (1 Timothy 2:1-4)

91

We Are Family

God not only answered our prayer but he generously invited others to be a part of this special day—the children present were blessed with encouraging words, music, and small gifts. Perhaps these children have shared this day with others in their lives. I hope they never forget what a beautiful visit this was, even when they are grown up. I do know one of the children, now a teenager, remembers this day and thinks of it often as a very special one.

I have shared this story with a few others, including a man who is blind. He listened intently to my telling of the story, and when I finished, he smiled the biggest smile. Although he could not see with his physical eyes, he was able to see with his spiritual eyes. This powerful drop of love continues to ripple outwards in its positive effects on others. Jesus is a loving God and He created a beautiful and unique response to our prayer that will continue to bless us and those around us.

92

Holy Harmony

When Robert (aka Jesus) gifted my daughter with the harmonica, I knew it was extra special and that I should make sure it was protected. I cleaned the harmonica after our guests left and both my daughter and I tried playing it later in the evening. It was a good quality harmonica and it played clearly. I couldn't help wondering if Jesus had played this harmonica while strolling through the countryside and cityscapes. Did he play a song on it for anyone along the way or did he play it when alone for his own enjoyment? Did the notes float through the air with special graces for all who heard them?

I stored the harmonica on a shelf with other musical instruments and books. I considered one day buying a special case for it, getting a label engraved and hanging it on the wall. But an instrument's purpose is to be played for the enjoyment of others.

I was contacted by a parent from DMCS who mentioned that her son had a part in the Christmas concert. His class was going to sing Silent Night and do a skit about the temporary peace between the Germans and the Allied soldiers at some of the front lines on Christmas Day 1914. The soldiers sang songs together, some played instruments, talked, and laughed, and there was an account of a game of soccer in the snow. The soldiers also used this time to retrieve the bodies of comrades who had fallen in the middle of the conflict before the temporary ceasefire. After the short reprieve, the soldiers on both sides went back to their call of duty.

This parent mentioned that she needed a harmonica for her son to play during the song the students would be singing. I quickly told her that I had a harmonica that her son could borrow. I let her know that it came from Someone very special and to please remind her son to handle it with care. I knew that He would want the harmonica to be played and to not sit on a shelf in silence. I knew the music would be filled with love for all in attendance.

How fitting that the Prince of Peace would have His gift played in a skit where the soldiers laid down their weapons and took on peace, love, and joy. Although it was only for a short time, it made a difference in the lives of these enemies who were given a chance to recognise each other's humanity.

93

Love Can Heal

Jesus had an encouraging and confirming word for me that summer day that has stayed with me and guided me since. He told me I was *on the right track*, and now that I know it was Jesus who spoke those words to me, I am reassured that I am doing His will in my life. This gives me great peace and hope as I continue on this special mission of sharing the Good News with others.

When Jesus shared the inspiring message about the Throne Room and the love that comes from God and goes out into the world and into families, it was a message that I could relate to, both in the past and the present. When He stated that if there is not enough love in the family there can be anger and depression, I could relate to that too. I think most people can recall times they did not feel loved whether growing up or as an adult.

Growing up in a large, busy family, I sometimes felt overlooked, misunderstood, and not appreciated. I was a sensitive child with deep feelings in a family of detached thinkers and I sometimes felt like I was "born into the wrong family." I didn't always feel like I fit in and yes, I didn't always feel loved. Whether that was because of the limitations of my parents, family dynamics, the times we grew up in, my temperament, misunderstandings with my siblings and parents, disagreements, unresolved issues, hurtful experiences, negative spiritual influences, or other reasons beyond the family such as with friends, school, or community, there was a definite lack of feeling loved a lot of the time. I grew up to become an adult with many hidden wounds—hidden even from myself.

This continued in the way my adult relationships were conducted. In search of love that I thought would complete me, it took me a very long time and many failed relationships to realize that the love I was in search of was God's love for me and a healthy love of myself as His beloved daughter. Once I learned to put God at the centre of my life, it ordered everything else in my life.

The enemy of our souls can also use these perceived or actual hurts to make us feel unworthy or to cause division. We can fixate on the lack of love in our past experiences. We can ruminate over hurtful situations and become stuck in the past. He is the "false accuser" and can influence our thoughts about ourselves and others. This is why it is so important to guard our thoughts and replace anything that is overly critical with more positive and loving thoughts. This also includes our words, intentions, and actions.

It took many years of struggle, heartache, learning, and growing to see the balm for my brokenness was in drawing closer to the Great Healer, Jesus. My deepening relationship with Jesus also helped me to forgive others; to understand some of their limitations and woundedness; to recall and appreciate all the good intentions of the people in my upbringing and adult life; to be thankful for the gifts, talents, opportunities, and experiences I was given; to develop healthy boundaries with others; to become more in touch with my own needs and desires; to take better care of myself, and to accept and love who I am.

> I praise you because I am fearfully and wonderfully made; your works are wonderful, I know that full well. (Psalm 139:14)

> ... 'Love the Lord your God with all your heart and with all your soul and with all your strength and with all your mind'; and, 'Love your neighbour *as yourself*.' (Luke 10:27)

It has been a journey of healing to wholeness, being grateful for the good in my life, accepting and moving on from what was not good, and making new and beautiful memories, one day at a time.

> For I know the plans I have for you," declares the Lord, "plans to prosper you and not to harm you, plans to give you hope and a future. (Jeremiah 29:11)

I am now very much aware of loving myself and others in a healthy and meaningful way. Whether through words or actions, I now put more effort into truly being present with love to those around me and those I encounter each day, without forgetting myself. I don't have to please anyone. I just love them in simple ways and seek to understand them as best I can. This approach has given me contentment and freedom to be who I am called to be.

This powerful message from Jesus is not only for me but for everyone to learn about and understand. Many people have struggled with not feeling enough love growing up or in their adult relationships and marriages. There may have been a deficit of love between their parents, in the parent-child relationships, between siblings, within the family as a whole, and with oneself. This may have continued to show up in their adult lives in different ways, including relationships, marriages, and new families.

> Do to others as you would have them do to you. (Luke 6:31)

Maybe it was...

- Inter-generational issues and cycles passed down that did not get resolved.
- Families where children's individual needs got overlooked.
- Careers that created mostly absent parents.
- Single-parent families with all of the added responsibilities.
- Foster family or adoptive family issues, or no real family.
- Financial stressors.
- Health issues—whether short-term or long-term.
- Employment and career issues.
- Mental health issues that didn't get treated, not well-treated, or difficult to treat.
- Addictions: alcohol, drugs, gambling, or others.
- Incarceration of parent or family member.
- Abuse whether physical, mental, emotional, or other.
- Death of a parent or family member.
- Relationship or marriage breakdown with all that can involve.
- Blended families that didn't always blend well.
- Grief, trauma or other wounds, including what has not been healed.
- Other circumstances not listed here that negatively impacted a person's life growing up, or as an adult.

These and others cause pain and sorrow that need understanding, forgiveness, and healing. We are all unique individuals and are each personally affected by our families of origin, including the parenting styles, sibling interactions, family dynamics, our upbringings, relationships, situations, circumstances, and experiences in our lives.

Some may require additional resources and professionals to assist with healing, such as counsellors, therapists, pastors, doctors, and other specialists. I encourage you to reach out for assistance from trusted and wise helpers and healers. There are many caring and knowledgeable people who are willing to help you deal with difficult issues, to recover, heal, and move forward in your life with hope.

This message has helped me to also see and understand the limitations that our parents, spouses, children, and family members have, and to be more accepting of everyone's shortcomings, including my own. We can forgive and move on with love. We can set and maintain healthy boundaries that ensure we are surrounded by people who understand, appreciate and care for us in positive, healthy and loving ways.

Many of us may genuinely love the people in our life, but we also need to express this love to them so they will truly know. I have tried my best to strive each day to be more loving to members of my family as well as to all the people I meet. It has also helped me to understand why so many people have had or continue to have struggles with their emotional and mental states, including with anger and depression. More love! We all need more love and we need to show more love to those around us and to those distant from us. Showing more love towards ourselves, our partner, our spouse, our children (including stepchildren and foster children), our parents and grandparents, our siblings, our relatives, our friends, our neighbours, our coworkers, our clients and customers, our community members, even strangers, can make a difference.

Let's all love a little better, starting today. Look around you at the people in your life. See the good in them. See their Creator's likeness in them. Now love them the best you can each and every day in thought, word, and action. It can be a kind word or note, listening to understand, a friendly hug, helping with a chore or errand, providing a drive, a small gift, an invitation to coffee(!), sharing a meal, or a special outing. Try to find ways to love them that they will appreciate. Remember to pray for them too!

Finding simple ways to include others is important to making them feel welcomed and loved, and it's good for us to be generous and compassionate towards them too. Think of ways you can practice *Conscious*

Caring by listening, speaking, or doing—with loving intentions. Remember the Source of Love and ask our loving God to pour His love into you and your family, and for it to flow out from there into the world for others.

The deepest healing for your wounded heart, mind, and soul is found in a simple yet complex answer: Love. Love is the healing remedy, God is the source of this love, and Jesus (God the Son) is the Divine Physician. Jesus can heal the hurt, soften the painful memories, take away the unhealthy anger, reduce and even remove the depression, and transform your life to give you hope and a brighter future. Once you are on your healing path, you can then share it with others around you. It will continue to flow out and impact others both near and far and perhaps inspire them on their journey.

> The Lord is close to the broken hearted and saves those who are crushed in spirit. (Psalm 34:18)

Jesus wants to set us free from feeling unworthy from not having all our needs met, or difficult experiences that made us feel less loved or unloved. We can start today with thinking about ourselves and others in the light of God's love for us all. Thinking beautiful and kind thoughts towards ourselves and others is the authentic way of loving ourselves, loving others and honouring the One who created us all. We can forgive, heal, and move on into a brighter future.

> Love is patient, love is kind. It does not envy, it does not boast, it is not proud. It does not dishonour others, it is not self-seeking, it is not easily angered, it keeps no record of wrongs. Love does not delight in evil but rejoices with the truth. It always protects, always trusts, always hopes, always perseveres. (1 Corinthians 13:4-7)

> Do everything in love. (1 Corinthians 16:14)

My command is this: Love each other as I have loved you. (John 15:12)

94

Do You Believe?

In recounting this story, I know there will be some people who will not believe it really happened or will not believe it was Jesus and Saint Michael who visited us that day. You have free will to believe or not to believe. This was a *private revelation* for me and the children. I have not approached any church about it nor do I have plans to have it undergo the rigours of examination by church authorities before I share it with others as that could take years, decades or longer, if at all! I think the world needs to hear this message TODAY!

I wonder how many private revelations over the years have been dismissed or not approved due to not quite enough proof. How many amazing encounters with the supernatural have gone undocumented? We live in a natural *and* supernatural world and amazing encounters and miracles are happening all the time all over the world.

This is a personal account of what I experienced five years ago and I have no need to prove my case to anyone. I know it really happened. I have the testimony of several children and adults who know Robert (aka Jesus) visited us. I had the experience confirmed by a wise gentleman with Gifts of the Holy Spirit. I have shared this encounter with other spiritually minded people and they have been open to the possibility of it having happened. Some have smiled and believed immediately, as though God whispered to their soul that *yes* He did come to visit us that day.

> ...because we look not at what can be seen but at what cannot be seen; for what can be seen is temporary, but what cannot be seen is eternal. (2 Corinthians 4:18)

No one would go to such an extent to time their meeting with me in front of a church after Mass, speak encouraging words, give messages with deep and personal meaning, speak of Heaven, and all the other positive actions like singing songs for us, showing the children the rosebush, picking up garbage, giving small gifts, and then be on their way. Who would do that and why? And Robert, aka Jesus, did what he said He would do. He did see me the following year at the summer conference and was with me at the AGM a couple of months after the conference.

Why would Jesus wear jeans? I think Jesus chose to be incognito with us that day and to try to blend in. Wearing one of the most common items of clothing would make sense if He was presenting himself as a regular stranger looking for coffee. It would not have worked as well if He appeared in a long, flowing robe or tunic. We would have probably recognized Him immediately. There have been many accounts of Jesus appearing in disguise throughout the world—as a beggar, homeless person, or other characters in the daily scenes of life. These are often for our testing and may be to intervene in a situation, to teach someone something important, to encourage and inspire. I know there have been a few times in my life where I thought the person or people I encountered were angels in disguise. How many other times have I really been meeting angels and didn't recognize it? I wonder if I ever met Jesus in disguise another time and did not realize it. It is a good reminder to treat everyone the same: with kindness, respect, and hospitality.

When I think that the God of the Universe was in my kitchen, I am humbled and in awe. I am also glad that my house was tidy that day! But God sees all and so He has also seen the dirty dishes and messy spaces on other days and He loves me the same. I am also reminded that Jesus was born in a cave as there was no place for Him at the time of His birth as His dear mother, the Virgin Mary, and His foster father, Saint Joseph, searched for a place but could find none. He lived a quiet, hidden life, learning the carpentry skills of his earthly father before His ministry officially began. He knew struggle, poverty, rejection, betrayal, pain, suffering and death.

He experienced much of what a human can, except sin. He is a Holy, humble and approachable God. I realize I don't have to cower in His presence, but a healthy *fear of the Lord* is appropriate, knowing God is the Creator and we are the created. To think, while I was making porridge, Jesus (God the Son) was powerfully present to everyone and everything in the world, because, as He had said, "God is everywhere." It moves me deeply that He who created the beautiful lands, mountains, oceans, animals, birds, fish, insects, bugs, trees, plants, flowers, sky, sun, moon, planets, stars, galaxies, and billions of people—took time to be with us that day. Jesus knows us better than we know ourselves. His love towards us is unchanging. He wants to be near His children. He wants us back in Heaven when our lives have finished here. He wants to love us forever—how amazing is that?

> ...yet for us there is but one God, the Father, from whom all things came and for whom we live; and there is but one Lord, Jesus Christ, through whom all things came and through whom we live. (1 Corinthians 8:6)

> For in him all things were created: things in heaven and on earth, visible and invisible, whether thrones or powers or rulers or authorities; all things have been created through him and for him. He is before all things, and in him all things hold together. (Colossians 1:16-17)

> We know also that the Son of God has come and has given us understanding, so that we may know him who is true. And we are in him who is true by being in his Son Jesus Christ. He is the true God and eternal life. (1 John 5:20)

Some might mention that Robert was wearing a wedding ring and said he was going back to his wife in Ontario. There was a lot of hidden symbolism in what Jesus was communicating that day. Jesus is known as the *bridegroom* and His church as the *bride*. We are invited to the *Wedding Supper of the Lamb* in Heaven where we will be united with Jesus forever. Maybe His next destination was going to be Ontario and He was going to visit more of His people there. After all, for God, Ontario is not that far away. He could make it there at the speed of light...or faster!

The repetition of Him having land in Nova Scotia is still a mystery to me, but I do think it is significant beyond my having relatives there and having lived and visited there. I have considered what it could mean but I will wait for His confirmation. I believe it will be revealed in God's perfect time and so I will wait on Him.

Why would Jesus visit me? In the eyes of the world I am no one special. But in the heart and mind of God, I am His beloved. I am unique and one of a kind. He created me and knows me. He answered my prayers and the prayers of my son and daughter with a visit. But as I have mentioned before, His visit had higher purposes and I believe His message was meant for sharing.

He was also in disguise and so the way he dressed and the things He spoke of were veiled in mystery. He decided that I would not completely recognize Him that day, although I did think it was something of Heaven and was hoping it was an angel or Jesus. Just like how in the Biblical story of *On The Road To Emmaus* Jesus did not allow Himself to be fully recognized until the breaking of the bread, He did not allow me to recognize Him until, with humility, courage, and faith, I shared my story with the man who has the Gift of Knowledge. Then my eyes were opened and with great joy I received in awe and wonder the Gift of that day! And the bonus was in knowing Saint Michael was with Him—the Commander of God's Army. Of note, on the day we met Robert and Elijah, and were walking to my home for coffee, I recall once we got into our line formation and were walking for a bit, Elijah (St. Michael) was at the head of the line beside me—just like I had confirmed: St. Michael always goes before Jesus! Amazing!

> While they were talking and discussing, Jesus himself came near and went with them, but their eyes were kept from recognizing him. (Luke 24:15-16)

> They said to each other, "Were not our hearts burning within us while he was talking to us on the road, while he was opening the scriptures to us?" (Luke 24:32)

As a side note, I did share what happened with a trusted priest and after I finished recounting the events he looked at me and said, "Truly, you have been blessed." He did not doubt and I believe God allowed him to know it was truly a visit from Him. Yes, I agree. I was blessed that day. I share this true story with you in the hopes that it blesses you too!

> For my thoughts are not your thoughts, nor are your ways my ways, says the Lord. For as the heavens are higher than the earth, so are my ways higher than your ways and my thoughts than your thoughts. (Isaiah 55:8-9)

95

All Things New

Jesus is always making things new. From a new day to a new love, new baby, new job, new house, new clothes, new cars, new friends, new trips, new hobbies, new experiences, *new* is a constant for the Great Creator. He wants to revive us from our stagnant lives and refresh us with good things—relationships, opportunities, and experiences. He also wants to renew His relationship with us.

God is not boring. Just look at His creation—the beauty of nature, variety of animals, colourful flowers, vast oceans, majestic mountains, the warmth and light of the sun, the night sky—all created for us, His children, to enjoy. Think about all the varieties of art, music, dance, sports, fitness, architecture, inventions, discoveries, food, vacation destinations, entertainment, pets, and people's unique lives! God has inspired individuals and groups over thousands of years to share their gifts and talents for the enjoyment and building up of our world. He wants each of us to continue to build up our part of the world to leave it better in some way, whether through loving our family and friends, serving in community organizations, financial gifts, volunteering, designing, building, creating art, making music—whether big or small, there is something we can all contribute to make a difference for those around us.

See the gift that is a new day. The next time you wake from your sleep, thank God: God the Father, God the Son, and God the Holy Spirit—three persons in one God, for a new day in your life, a fresh canvas on which you can create your masterpiece. Create something beautiful for you and others and sign it with your love. Someday it will hang in the Great Gallery of Your Life in Heaven.

> And the one who was seated on the throne said, "See, I am making all things new." Also he said, "Write this, for these words are trustworthy and true." (Revelation 21:5)

96

Jesus Is

Here are fifty observations of Jesus from the time I spent with Him:

1. Jesus is approachable.
2. Jesus has natural good looks.
3. Jesus has brown hair.
4. Jesus has brown eyes. (While in disguise.)
5. Jesus likes wearing jeans and jean jackets.
6. Jesus wears sandals. (Just like when he lived on the earth.)
7. Jesus is tall. (About 6 ft.)
8. Jesus is regal. (Even when in disguise.)
9. Jesus is quiet.
10. Jesus is polite.
11. Jesus is humble.
12. Jesus is friendly.
13. Jesus is a good listener.
14. Jesus is gentle.
15. Jesus is creative.
16. Jesus is adventurous.
17. Jesus is cool, very cool without trying to be cool.

18. Jesus likes coffee. He created coffee beans!
19. Jesus is patient.
20. Jesus is observant.
21. Jesus likes to give hugs.
22. Jesus knows me well.
23. Jesus is a great guitar player.
24. Jesus is a great singer.
25. Jesus is a great songwriter.
26. Jesus speaks with authority.
27. Jesus is wise.
28. Jesus meets us where we are.
29. Jesus sees our hurt.
30. Jesus wants us to have enough love.
31. Jesus loves all of His children whether young or grown-up.
32. Jesus loves flowers and wants us to enjoy them too.
33. Jesus is pure-hearted.
34. Jesus is active.
35. Jesus is considerate.
36. Jesus does not want litter on the earth.
37. Jesus does not want sin but right living.
38. Jesus only uses enough words to get His point across.
39. Jesus is present to you.
40. Jesus does not force but invites.
41. Jesus is always in search of the lost.
42. Jesus is lively.
43. Jesus is efficient with time.
44. Jesus is relational.
45. Jesus is a great teacher.
46. Jesus likes to travel.
47. Jesus is a great mystery of love.
48. Jesus wants us to grow in love.
49. Jesus has a plan for our lives.
50. Jesus wants us to go to Heaven.

I am not sure if Jesus likes porridge, but I know St. Michael does!

97

Confirmations

Important confirmations I received:

- God is real.
- Jesus is God.
- God heard our prayers!
- I am on the right track.
- Sunbeams is where the Son beamed!
- I am on the right path to Heaven.
- I am God's beloved daughter.
- God is pleased with my sharing of the Good News.
- Robert was Jesus Christ in disguise.
- Elijah was St. Michael the Archangel in disguise.
- God loves me.

98

Important To Remember

Here are a few important points for us all to remember:

- Daily Mass can make an ordinary day extraordinary.
- Be nice to strangers.
- If you meet a musician, ask for a song.
- Music connects people.
- Invite others into your church.
- Listen for important messages.
- Invite others for coffee.
- Be hospitable.
- Don't litter.
- Do your part to keep your neighbourhood clean.
- Sinning negatively affects the planet.
- Do the right thing all the time.
- Follow Jesus' (God's) teachings.
- God has a plan for each of us.
- God is guiding us.
- Look out for your neighbour.
- Seek fellowship.
- Be generous.

- Stay open to possibilities.
- Receive the gift being offered.
- Search and you will find.
- Be humble.
- Ask for assistance.
- Feeling depressed or angry might be related to a lack of love.
- Love your spouse in an extra special way.
- Show your children you love them.
- Express love as a family.
- Fill your home with love.
- Trust your gut.
- Be hopeful for the future.
- Jesus loves everyone.
- Expect the unexpected.
- God is love.
- Love comes from God.
- God is everywhere.

> And now these three remain: faith, hope and love.
> But the greatest of these is love.
> (1 Corinthians 13:13)

99

An Invitation For You

I would like to invite you to an amazing place where you will be supremely happy forever. This is a place that has already been prepared for you. The One who prepared it knows you better than you know yourself. He has created the perfect space filled with all that will satisfy, surprise, and delight you. It is filled with beautiful places, special treasures and amazing experiences that will fill you with wonder. Most importantly you will feel a powerful love all the time. You will never be sad again, nor mad—no anger, depression, anxiety or worry—just PEACE, JOY, and LOVE. All the former things will fade away and be replaced with the Eternal Day that will more than satisfy you and provide great contentment and joy. All you have to do is RSVP. It's that simple. Just send your response by praying these 12 words aloud with all your heart, mind, and soul:

Jesus Prayer:

Lord Jesus Christ, Son of God, have mercy on me, a sinner.

100

Next Steps

Congratulations! You did it. Your place in Heaven has been reserved for you! Now, you want to make sure you have made yourself ready and will be welcomed. This is such a beautiful and special place. All who have already arrived have made themselves ready. It took some extra effort but it was worth it in the end. The most important thing to remember is that God is Love. He wants you to love Him, love others, and love yourself. He wants you to turn away from all that is not right in your life. He wants you to become holy, like Him. You can do it. Start today, right now. If you fall, get up, dust yourself off and begin again. Here are a few ways to start on your journey to Jesus and Heaven:

Ask Jesus what church He would like you to attend. He will lead you in a recognizable way. Then start going to church each week. You will discover a supportive community.

Get a Bible and read from it each day. It will give you special insights and help for your life.

Learn more about Jesus and His laws of love and life.

Spend quiet time in prayer each day. Prayer is a conversation. You can speak with Jesus. He is a good listener and He loves to hear from His people. You can also speak to God the Father, and God the Holy Spirit or all three divine persons, the Holy Trinity – together they are one God.

Keep showing up and you will see God move in your life.

Stay strong and courageous.

Remember the final prize which is Heaven. Heaven is your homeland!

Jesus is the Way, the Truth, and the Life!

> Love has been perfected among us in this: that we may have boldness on the day of judgement, because as he is, so are we in this world. There is no fear in love, but perfect love casts out fear; for fear has to do with punishment, and whoever fears has not reached perfection in love. We love because he first loved us. (John 4:17-19)

101

Be Wise

> If any of you is lacking in wisdom, ask God, who gives to all generously and ungrudgingly, and it will be given you. (James 1:5)

A few words of caution as you navigate your life here on the earth in the near future. There is coming a time when Christians are going to be despised, and unfortunately it has already arrived for many people in different parts of the world. We will be persecuted for our faith as the battle for souls continues. Just as Jesus suffered, we will too. Maybe not as a martyr but in other ways that make life difficult. Please remember to be courageous and strong. Strive to please God and offer your sacrifices and sufferings to Him.

Be careful of what Bible you use. Some of the newer versions might skew the meaning of certain scriptures. Study your Bible well so you know what God expects of you and so that you will not be deceived by what others may say that could mislead you. If anyone tries to convince you of something that is against Holy Scriptures, you will be ready to refuse.

Jesus is the same yesterday, today and forever. Although He makes all things new, there is still a constancy about Him and His teachings that can never be modernized or adapted to suit the changing whims of the world. His ways of love and life are timeless treasures. Follow them and you will have deep and abiding peace.

Be careful of "wolves in sheep's clothing" whether in a church, in leadership, business, your family, relatives, friends and neighbours. Ask yourself if what they are saying aligns with Christ's teachings. If not, then you are not required to listen nor follow them. Pray for them that they will see the error of their ways. You will know them by their fruits. Bad fruit or good fruit? Pay attention and this simple test will give you the answer.

> **A Tree and Its Fruit**
> 'Beware of false prophets, who come to you in sheep's clothing but inwardly are ravenous wolves. You will know them by their fruits. Are grapes gathered from thorns, or figs from thistles? In the same way, every good tree bears good fruit, but the bad tree bears bad fruit. A good tree cannot bear bad fruit, nor can a bad tree bear good fruit. Every tree that does not bear good fruit is cut down and thrown into the fire. Thus you will know them by their fruits. (Matthew 7:15-20)

Avoid any New World Religion that tries to lump together several religions under one banner. You cannot take several different faiths and try to make them all true. IT WILL NOT WORK! Don't be fooled! Jesus is the Way, the Truth, and the Life! Jesus is the one and only Saviour of the World. Jesus is God! God had to come down to earth, suffer and die a cruel death on a wooden cross to redeem us. The stakes are very high for the salvation of your soul. Take it seriously because it *is* VERY SERIOUS.

> Jesus answered, "I am the way and the truth and the life. No one comes to the Father except through me. If you really know

me, you will know my Father as well. From now on, you do know him and have seen him." (John 14:6-7)

Keep alert to schism in the church which will result in divisions and factions. Follow the true church that keeps the original faith and its teachings. Know the Sacred Scriptures and Sacred Traditions of the church and follow them. Familiarize yourself with the Magisterium of the Church. Do not follow any new teachings that subvert the Word of God and the traditions that have been handed down over the course of two thousand years. They are tried and true!

If the teachings or important prayers at your church begin to change and you no longer feel comfortable there, it is time to move. If what you are hearing is not the truth passed down from generations before you, nor what is in a trusted Bible, find another church. If you have to go 'underground' to find a church that you can trust, choose wisely. Pray about it.

In the end, the most important thing you have is your SOUL. That is all that is leaving this world when you depart from it. Guard and protect it and make it spotless and ready for Heaven.

> **Concerning Treasures**
> 'Do not store up for yourselves treasures on earth, where moth and rust consume and where thieves break in and steal; but store up for yourselves treasures in heaven, where neither moth nor rust consumes and where thieves do not break in and steal. For where your treasure is, there your heart will be also.

Remember to always follow Jesus. Choose to always please God, not man. God should be first in your life!

> **There Is No Other Gospel**
> I am astonished that you are so quickly deserting the one who called you in the grace of Christ and are turning to a different

> gospel—not that there is another gospel, but there are some who are confusing you and want to pervert the gospel of Christ. But even if we or an angel from heaven should proclaim to you a gospel contrary to what we proclaimed to you, let that one be accursed! As we have said before, so now I repeat, if anyone proclaims to you a gospel contrary to what you received, let that one be accursed! Am I now seeking human approval, or God's approval? Or am I trying to please people? If I were still pleasing people, I would not be a servant of Christ. (Galatians 1:6-10)

Share the Good News with others in your life! Whether you have had Jesus in your life for a few years, many years, all of it or if you have just started your journey, please don't keep it to yourself. Remember to pass the Torch to others so they can have the Light of Christ in their lives too! Share what Jesus means to you, and how He has helped you in your life. Share a Bible scripture passage, a prayer, and a few words of hope. Invite them to church, a Bible Study, or other activity or event at your church. You *can* make a difference in someone's life, especially their eternal life. Give the free gift of faith, hope and love today!

> Therefore, since we are surrounded by such a great cloud of witnesses, let us throw off everything that hinders and the sin that so easily entangles. And let us run with perseverance the race marked out for us, fixing our eyes on Jesus, the pioneer and perfecter of faith. For the joy set before him he endured the cross, scorning its shame, and sat down at the right hand of the throne of God. Consider him who endured such opposition from sinners, so that you will not grow weary and lose heart. (Hebrews 12:1-3)

ADDENDUM

A-1

Do Not Quench the Spirit

Do not quench the Spirit.
Do not despise the words of prophets, but test everything;
hold fast to what is good;
(1 Thessalonians 5: 19-21)

A-2

Final Note

Dear reader,

I hope that you enjoyed reading about the encounter I had with strangers whose real identity was heaven-sent. It is a reminder to always treat everyone we meet with kindness because we just might one day be *entertaining angels* or even God! If we continue to seek the light that is in each other and honour that, we can discover the many facets of truth, beauty, and goodness that God has put there. If we all lay down our weapons—many that are invisible—and replace them with the power of love, we will begin to see changes in ourselves, our families, communities and beyond. One drop of love can ripple throughout the world.

Love one another, for Love comes from God. (Jesus, who is God, told me so Himself.)

> And so we know and rely on the love God has for us. God is love. Whoever lives in love lives in God, and God in them.
> (1 John 4:16)

With love,
Vita Marie Kipping

A-3

Afterword

This experience helped me to know how close God really is—that He is near to us, listens to us, loves us and cares about our everyday lives. God delights in His creation including His children of all ages: the unborn, infants, toddlers, young children, youth, adults, seniors, and the elderly. He is watching over you. He is a Good Father.

It also reminded me of the power of prayer and that if we step forward with expectant Faith, God will respond. He does not force us but wants us to draw closer to Him in freedom and love. He is just a prayer away. He will also meet you at church; in the stillness and quiet; through praise music (even in your kitchen); in reading Bible scripture; in the faces of the poor, the sick, the homeless, and the stranger.

He wants us to be healed of all that has wounded us. He wants us to become whole through love, His love. His love has transformed lives and will continue to for all eternity. Time will eventually run out for each of us on the earth but if we believe and follow Jesus, we will be welcomed into the most perfect, timeless place—Heaven—prepared for those who truly love. Every day presents many opportunities to love—to love God, love your neighbour, and love yourself. Love is the way that leads to healing, hope and Heaven.

Remember you came from Love, to know Love, to fulfill your special mission on earth, and to return to the Kingdom of Love (Heaven). God has prepared a beautiful and amazing place for you in Heaven and He is expecting you. This is going to be the Best Homecoming!

    I wonder if there will be coffee in Heaven.

A-4

Scriptures On Hospitality

Do not neglect to show hospitality to strangers, for thereby some have entertained angels unawares. (Hebrews 13:2)

Show hospitality to one another without grumbling. (1 Peter 4:9)

Contribute to the needs of the saints and seek to show hospitality. (Romans 12:13)

"You shall treat the stranger who sojourns with you as the native among you, and you shall love him as yourself, for you were strangers in the land of Egypt: I am the Lord your God." (Leviticus 19:34)

But hospitable, a lover of good, self-controlled, upright, holy, and disciplined. (Titus 1:8)

Whoever speaks, as one who speaks oracles of God; whoever serves, as one who serves by the strength that God supplies—in order that in everything God may be glorified through Jesus Christ. To him belong glory and dominion forever and ever. Amen. (1 Peter 4:11)

And having a reputation for good works: if she has brought up children, has shown hospitality, has washed the feet of the saints, has cared for the afflicted, and has devoted herself to every good work. (1 Timothy 5:10)

One day Elisha went on to Shunem, where a wealthy woman lived, who urged him to eat some food. So whenever he passed that way, he would turn in there to eat food. (2 Kings 4:8)

Beloved, it is a faithful thing you do in all your efforts for these brothers, strangers as they are. (3 John 1:5)

And after she was baptized, and her household as well, she urged us, saying, "If you have judged me to be faithful to the Lord, come to my house and stay." And she prevailed upon us. (Acts 16:15)

The islanders showed us unusual kindness. They built a fire and welcomed us all because it was raining and cold. (Acts 28:2)

Rendering service with a good will as to the Lord and not to man. (Ephesians 6:7)

"You shall not wrong a sojourner or oppress him, for you were sojourners in the land of Egypt." (Exodus 22:21)

For you were called to freedom, brothers. Only do not use your freedom as an opportunity for the flesh, but through love serve one another. (Galatians 5:13)

So then, as we have opportunity, let us do good to everyone, and especially to those who are of the household of faith. (Galatians 6:10)

Do not neglect to do good and to share what you have, for such sacrifices are pleasing to God. (Hebrews 13:16)

"Is it not to share your bread with the hungry and bring the homeless poor into your house; when you see the naked, to cover him, and not to hide yourself from your own flesh?" (Isaiah 58:7)

The sojourner has not lodged in the street; I have opened my doors to the traveler. (Job 31:32)

"And you shall not strip your vineyard bare, neither shall you gather the fallen grapes of your vineyard. You shall leave them for the poor and for the sojourner: I am the Lord your God." (Leviticus 19:10)

"When a stranger sojourns with you in your land, you shall not do him wrong." (Leviticus 19:33)

She opens her hand to the poor and reaches out her hands to the needy. (Proverbs 31:20)

Now as they went on their way, Jesus entered a village. And a woman named Martha welcomed him into her house. (Luke 10:38)

"And the King will answer them, 'Truly, I say to you, as you did it to one of the least of these my brothers, you did it to me." (Matthew 25:40)

Then Jesus said to his host, "When you give a luncheon or dinner, do not invite your friends, your brothers or sisters, your relatives, or your rich neighbors; if you do, they may invite you back and so you will be repaid. But when you give a banquet, invite the poor, the crippled, the lame, the blind, and you will be blessed. Although they cannot repay you, you will be repaid at the resurrection of the righteous." (Luke 14:12-14)

A-5

Confirming One's Calling and Election

His divine power has given us everything we need for a godly life through our knowledge of him who called us by his own glory and goodness. Through these he has given us his very great and precious promises, so that through them you may participate in the divine nature, having escaped the corruption in the world caused by evil desires.

For this very reason, make every effort to add to your faith goodness; and to goodness, knowledge; and to knowledge, self-control; and to self-control, perseverance; and to perseverance, godliness; and to godliness, mutual affection; and to mutual affection, **love**. For if you possess these qualities in increasing measure, they will keep you from being ineffective and unproductive in your knowledge of our Lord Jesus Christ. But whoever does not have them is nearsighted and blind, forgetting that they have been cleansed from their past sins.

Therefore, my brothers and sisters, make every effort to confirm your calling and election. For if you do these things, you will never stumble, and you will receive a **rich welcome into the eternal kingdom of our Lord and Saviour Jesus Christ.** (2 Peter 1:3-11)

A-6

Psalm 45

The Glories of the Messiah and His Bride

To the Chief Musician. Set to "The Lilies." A Contemplation of the sons of Korah. A Song of Love.

My heart is overflowing with a good theme;

I recite my composition concerning the King;

My tongue is the pen of a ready writer.

You are fairer than the sons of men;

Grace is poured upon Your lips;

Therefore God has blessed You forever.

Gird Your sword upon Your thigh, O Mighty One,

With Your glory and Your majesty.

And in Your majesty ride prosperously because of truth, humility, and righteousness;

And Your right hand shall teach You awesome things.

Your arrows are sharp in the heart of the King's enemies;

The peoples fall under You.

Your throne, O God, is forever and ever;

A scepter of righteousness is the scepter of Your kingdom.

You love righteousness and hate wickedness;

Therefore God, Your God, has anointed You

With the oil of gladness more than Your companions.

All Your garments are scented with myrrh and aloes and cassia,

Out of the ivory palaces, by which they have made You glad.

Kings' daughters are among Your honourable women;

At Your right hand stands the queen in gold from Ophir.

Listen, O daughter,

Consider and incline your ear;

Forget your own people also, and your father's house;

So the King will greatly desire your beauty;

Because He is your Lord, worship Him.

And the daughter of Tyre will come with a gift;

The rich among the people will seek your favour.

The royal daughter is all glorious within the palace;

Her clothing is woven with gold.

She shall be brought to the King in robes of many colours;

The virgins, her companions who follow her, shall be brought to You.

With gladness and rejoicing they shall be brought;

They shall enter the King's palace.

Instead of Your fathers shall be Your sons,

Whom You shall make princes in all the earth.

I will make Your name to be remembered in all generations;

Therefore the people shall praise You forever and ever.

A-7

I Am Coming Soon

"Look, I am coming soon! My reward is with me, and I will give to each person according to what they have done. I am the Alpha and the Omega, the First and the Last, the Beginning and the End.

"Blessed are those who wash their robes, that they may have the right to the tree of life and may go through the gates into the city. Outside are the dogs, those who practice magic arts, the sexually immoral, the murderers, the idolaters and everyone who loves and practices falsehood.

The Spirit and the bride say, "Come!" And let the one who hears say, "Come!" Let the one who is thirsty come; and let the one who wishes take the free gift of the water of life. (Revelation 22:12-17)

He who testifies to these things says,

"Surely I am coming quickly."

Amen. Even so, come, Lord Jesus!

(Revelation 22:20)

... "Everyone who calls on the name of the Lord will be saved."
(Romans 10:13)

Coffee In The Clouds .ca

Vita Marie Kipping

Vita Marie Kipping was born and raised in Saint John, New Brunswick, on the east coast of Canada, ten minutes from the ocean. She left home at 18 for university in Halifax, Nova Scotia, then went to Toronto, Ontario for college and work for several years. Her background is in graphic design, communications, marketing, project management, training, office administration, and childcare enrichment. Vita loved reading stories to her children when they were little and making up bedtime stories on the spot. She enjoys writing, listening to music, reading, creating art, sewing, decorating, gardening, road trips, hot drinks and chatting with people she meets on the street. She lives with her family and fur baby in Saint John—the place she will always call home. **Coffee In The Clouds** is her second published book (2023). Her first book, **To The Other Side Of The World: In The Aftermath Of 9-11**, was published in 2021.

www.ingramcontent.com/pod-product-compliance
Lightning Source LLC
Chambersburg PA
CBHW070643120526
44590CB00013BA/837